NORFOLK TERR

TAIL
Medium docked.

LOIN
Strong.

THIGH
Strong and muscular.

HOCKS
Well let down and straight.

FEET
Round with thick pads.

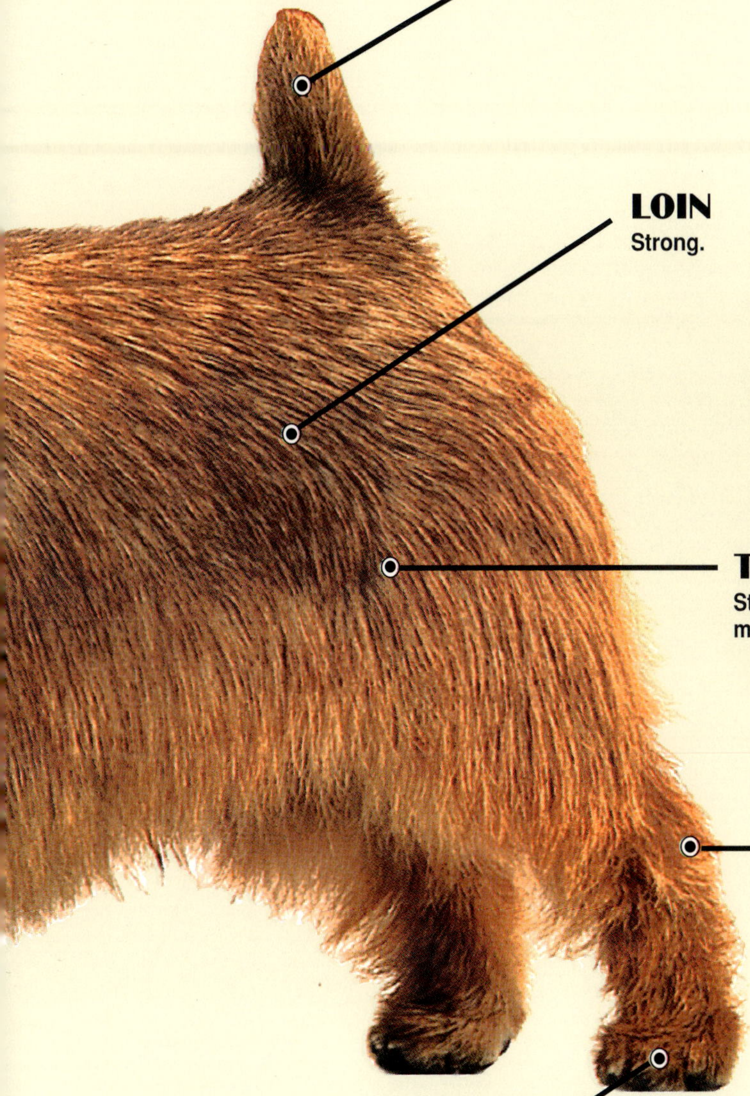

Title page: Ch. Nanfan's Crunch owned by Mrs. Barbara Miller.

Photographers: John Ashbey, Mary Bloom, Booth Photography, W. Bushman, Callea Photo, Donna Coss, Judith Felton, Isabelle Francais, Judy Iby, Margaret Miller, Michele Perlmutter, Gregory Siner.

© **by T.F.H. Publications, Inc.**

Distributed in the UNITED STATES to the Pet Trade by T.F.H. Publications, Inc., One T.F.H. Plaza, Neptune City, NJ 07753; distributed in the UNITED STATES to the Bookstore and Library Trade by National Book Network, Inc. 4720 Boston Way, Lanham MD 20706; in CANADA to the Pet Trade by H & L Pet Supplies Inc., 27 Kingston Crescent, Kitchener, Ontario N2B 2T6; Rolf C. Hagen Inc., 3225 Sartelon St. Laurent-Montreal Quebec H4R 1E8; in CANADA to the Book Trade by Vanwell Publishing Ltd., 1 Northrup Crescent, St. Catharines, Ontario L2M 6P5 ; in ENGLAND by T.F.H. Publications, PO Box 15, Waterlooville PO7 6BQ; in AUSTRALIA AND THE SOUTH PACIFIC by T.F.H. (Australia), Pty. Ltd., Box 149, Brookvale 2100 N.S.W., Australia; in NEW ZEALAND by Brooklands Aquarium Ltd. 5 McGiven Drive, New Plymouth, RD1 New Zealand; in Japan by T.F.H. Publications, Japan—Jiro Tsuda, 10-12-3 Ohjidai, Sakura, Chiba 285, Japan; in SOUTH AFRICA by Lopis (Pty) Ltd., P.O. Box 39127, Booysens, 2016, Johannesburg, South Africa. Published by T.F.H. Publications, Inc.

MANUFACTURED IN THE
UNITED STATES OF AMERICA
BY T.F.H. PUBLICATIONS, INC.

NORFOLK TERRIER

A COMPLETE AND RELIABLE HANDBOOK

Anna Katherine Nicholas

RX-111

CONTENTS

Description of the Norfolk Terrier 7

Evolution of the Norfolk Terrier 12
Development in Great Britain

The Norfolk Terrier as a Pet 21
Activities for You and Your Norfolk Terrier

Grooming Your Norfolk Terrier 30

Your Puppy's New Home 37
On Arriving Home • Dangers in the Home • The First Night •
Other Pets • Housetraining • The Early Days • Identification

Feeding Your Norfolk Terrier 50
Factors Affecting Nutritional Needs • Composition and Role
of Food • Amount to Feed • When to Feed

Training Your Norfolk Terrier 59
Collar and Leash Training • The Sit Command • The Come
Command • The Heel Command • The Stay Command •
The Down Command • Recall to Heel Command • The No Command

Your Healthy Norfolk Terrier 68
Physical Exam • Healthy Teeth and Gums • Fighting Fleas •
The Trouble with Ticks • Insects and Other Outdoor Dangers •
Skin Disorders • Internal Disorders • Worms • Bloat
(Gastric Dilatation) • Vaccinations • Accidents

Congenital and Acquired Disorders 84
Bones and Joints • Cardiovascular and Lymphatic Systems • Blood •
Digestive System and Oral Cavity • Endocrine System • Eyes •
Neuromuscular System • Urogenital

DESCRIPTION OF THE NORFOLK TERRIER

There is still confusion in the minds of many dog fanciers who are new to these breeds about the difference in type that exist between Norfolk and Norwich Terriers. True, they both go back to the same size and colors. But, as time has passed, obvious differences have emerged.

In the beginning, it was assumed that all these small red dogs were related to one another and that all were generally the same basic terrier, with the only difference being the carriage of the ears. As time

The Norfolk is a terrier that was bred to be a sturdy little dog of unquestioned courage and tenacity. Max-Well's Winter Thyme owned by Mrs. Barbara Miller.

DESCRIPTION

The definite differences between the two types of Norwich Terriers soon lead to the recognition of the Norfolk as a separate breed. Ch. Max-Well's Weatherman owned by Mrs. Barbara Miller.

progressed, various other subtle differences started to surface and gradually the realization took over that the drop-eared type of Norwich Terrier definitely was not, except for the ear carriage, an exact duplicate of the Norwich Terrier. Quite the contrary, one learned on thoughtful observation.

When the Norwich Terrier first received official recognition and admittance to the Kennel Club of Great Britain during the early 1930s, there were a number with the pendant (drop) ears intermixed with those whose ears were upright. Additionally, there were others who actually did have drop ears that had been altered in appearance by cropping. In the early days it was quite customary to interbreed dogs of these different ear carriages, which led to somewhat of a mishmash as far as type was concerned.

Gradually things changed. Fanciers became increasingly aware that they were dealing with not two types of dog within a breed but with two distinct breeds. This realization was first achieved in England in 1964, then in the United States in 1979, with recognition of the Norfolk. On both of these occasions new standards for Norfolk Terriers, separate from the Norwich standards, were drawn up, and gradually the handsome little Norfolks that we know today emerged.

DESCRIPTION

The Norfolk Terrier as we know the breed today is small and rough-coated, measuring nine to ten inches in height at the withers and weighing in at around 11–12 pounds at maturity. The weight should be appropriate for the structure, balance and condition of the animal, with fitness and working condition being of utmost importance.

The length of the back from point of withers to base of tail of the Norfolk Terrier should measure slightly longer than the height at withers. The ribs are well sprung (nicely rounded), chest moderately deep, topline level and the loins strong.

AmEng. Ch. Clockwise of Jaeva owned by Mrs. Barbara Miller shows the characteristic drop ears that distinguishes the breed.

The skull is wide, rounded slightly, with good width between the ears. The muzzle should be about one-third of the total length of head when measured from occiput to stop (the well-defined hollow between the eyes) and from stop to tip of nose.

The ears are small, neatly dropped, with a break at the skull line, carried close to the cheek and falling no lower than the outer corner of the eye. Slightly rounded at the tip, the ears are V-shaped and feel smooth and velvety to the touch.

The eyes are small, dark and oval, surrounded by black eye rims. They are bright and sparkling, placed well apart, with keen intelligent expression.

DESCRIPTION

The jaw is clean and strong, lips are tight, large teeth meeting in a scissors bite.

The Norfolk's neck is strong and of medium length, blending smoothly into well laid-back shoulders. Chest of good width. Elbows carried close to ribs, pasterns strong. Short, powerful forelegs should be as straight as is consistent with the digging terrier.

The hindquarters are broad, thighs strong and muscular. Good turn of thighs and well let-down hocks providing the drive to work smoothly with the equally strong reach of forelegs. Hocks straight when viewed from behind.

Norfolk feet are round with thick pads, toenails strong and black. The tail is straight and set on high, medium, docked to a length to assure a balanced outline.

The outer (protective) coat is hard, wiry and straight, about an inch and a half to two inches in length, lying close to the body and with a dense undercoat. Longer mane on neck and shoulders also forms a ruff at the base of the ears and throat. Moderate furnishing on the legs are of harsh texture. Head and ears covered with short, smooth hair except for slight eyebrows and whiskers. The dog should be tidied only sufficiently to look neat. In the show ring, shaping, or sculpting should be penalized severely.

The Norfolk's outer coat is hard, wiry and straight with a dense undercoat and a longer mane around the neck and shoulders. Owner, Mrs. Barbara Miller.

DESCRIPTION

Ch. Max-Well's Blizzard with handler Susan Kipp winning Best of Winners.

Norfolk colors are all shades of red, wheaten, black and tan, or grizzle. Dark points are permissible; white marks are undesirable.

The little Norfolk moves with strength and assurance. Gait true, low and driving. Forelegs extend forward from the shoulders; rear angulation providing strong powerful propulsion from behind. Viewed in profile from the side, hind legs follow in the tracks of the forelegs, moving smoothly from the hip and flexing well at the stifle and hock. Topline remains level as the dog moves along.

As your knowledge and familiarity with both breeds continues to grow, you will become increasingly aware of the differences between the Norfolk and the Norwich—especially the Norfolk ears, of course. In general conformation, the Norfolk is a bit different, too, as these little fellows are somewhat angular in appearance. They have larger feet, are slightly longer in neck and loin, and tend to have better angulation in the hindquarters.

EVOLUTION OF THE NORFOLK TERRIER

For many centuries on the farms of Great Britain, small, hardy, industrious little dogs, members of the terrier family, earned respect for their proficiency and expertise in keeping the rodent population under control. These little dogs were invaluable in the service performed.

Among the most popular, and probably the very smallest of the various British terrier types, was a strain of deep red, rough-coated dogs, sometimes also seen in black and tan, who were to be found making themselves useful as co-inhabitants with the horses and the sporting hounds. Being small and short legged, these little fellows were able to enter many holes and burrows into which larger dogs could not make the grade, and thus were particularly useful for bolting rats, foxes, and whatever. The red dogs were sufficiently similar in traits and appearance to be

The many faces of Ch. Rightly So Original Sin as painted by M. Van Loan. Owners, Mrs. W. Hedges and Julius Rumpf.

EVOLUTION

considered of a single "family"—a belief that long survived until our present century when the breeding of dogs reached new heights and became more specialized.

It did not take long for the value of these dogs and their efficiency to be realized, attracting the attention of people interested not only in their fearlessness and hardy ability to hold their own when working, but also in the possible financial gain they might involve.

For example, one "Doggy" Lawrence, so named due to his involvement with the little canines, gained fame and I am sure at least a reasonable amount of

An infamous Norfolk Terrier from the 1930s, Gypsy Queen at three months old. Photo courtesy of Barbara Miller.

fortune by providing and selling little red terriers to the undergraduates at Cambridge University who used them as pit-fighters against rats, as ratters, and, in some cases, as pets.

At the turn of the century and into the 1900s came the person who had, without a doubt, the greatest amount of individual influence on the future of these

EVOLUTION

Ch. Badgewood Brackeu owned by Mrs. Phillip S.P. Fell winning a Best of Breed in 1978 under famous terrier judge William Kendrick.

small red terriers. This was Frank Jones, more popularly known as "Roughrider Jones" due to his expertise in the training and handling of horses. Mr. Jones became so closely associated with the small feisty dogs that soon they were being identified as "Jones Terriers," a name that remained with them not only in Great Britain but in America as well.

To fill in a bit of biography on Mr. Jones, he originally came from Ireland, from County Wickwire, accompanied by a pair of small bright red terriers. He boasted quite a reputation for his success at training "green" horses with several Foxhound packs, and his first position in 1901 was as whip to the Norwich Foxhounds in the employment of Master J.E. Cooke. Mr. Jones was 25 years old at the time.

As it happened, M. Cooke's estate was near a livery stable owned by E. Jodrell Hopkins, where small stable terriers were kept; these dogs were known as Trumpingham Terriers in honor of the street in Cam-

EVOLUTION

Colonsay won a host of friends, among them some very noted and respected names in British dog-show lore.

It was in 1933 that Sheila Macfie met her first drop-eared Norwich. She became probably the most determined crusader of all for separate classifications for the two ear types of Norwich Terriers and suffered defeats along the way. What a happy triumph for her when, having started this campaign in 1957, victory was finally attained several years later with even more than originally hoped for—complete separation into two breeds for the drop-eared, now known as the Norfolk, and the prick-eared Norwich. (The United States followed suit 14 years later.)

The Colonsay drop-ears furnished foundation stock for several leading lines, among them such noted English strains as Hunston, Ickworth, Ragus, Ravenswing, and Rabincott and in the United States, Bethway, Kedron, Partree and Port Fortune.

A number of other kennels have played their part in the progress of the drop-eared Norwich Terrier in the early days. Alice Hazeldine with her Ickworths was a

Opposite: Ch. Nanfan Crunch owned by Mrs. Barbara Miller is a product of the Nanfan Kennels, a name that has gained an important part in Norfolk history due to the excellence and quality of their dogs.

A shining example of the breed, Ch. Rightly So Original Sin owned by Mrs. W. Hedges and Julius Rumpf gained many admirers during his successful show career.

EVOLUTION

AmEng. Ch. Jaeva Matti Brown owned by Mrs. Barbara Miller.

first standard for the breed was approved in 1935. Of course, differences persisted regarding the prick ears versus the drop ear, each type having its sincere supporters and followers.

Marion Sheila Scott Macfie of Colonsay Kennels was one of the greatest friends of the drop-eared Norwich Terriers. These were her favorites, and her enthusiasm knew no bounds, nor did her efforts to see them gain their own separate listing. When World War II broke out, this lady placed some of her finest breeding stock on farms of friends in East Angzia, where she felt they would be safe; at the same time, she sent at least two pairs of her finest drop-ears to Percy Roberts in the United States for placement with clients who would look to their future.

At the close of the War, Miss Macfie took her drop-eared Norwich Terriers to numerous shows along with her famous team of Dalmatians. In the variety classes, where they competed, the drop-eareds from

EVOLUTION

Foundations of the "Jones Terriers" came, therefore, from Rags and from the dogs who had accompanied Mr. Jones from Ireland and their various progeny.

Eventually Mr. Jones moved to Market Harborough, where he remained for the rest of his life. When he was leaving Norwich, he was asked how he identified his pack of terriers to which he replied "Norwich Terriers," thus naming the breed—although the identification "Jones Terriers" had stuck with them over a long period of time in both Great Britain and the United States.

DEVELOPMENT IN GREAT BRITAIN

By the start of the 1930s, attempts were under way on the part of various Norwich Terrier owners to

An influential member of the Norfolk Terrier breed, Ch. Badgewood Monty Collins met with much success as both a show and stud dog. Owner, Mrs. Phillip S.P. Fell.

achieve official Kennel Club recognition for their dogs. Frank Jones, incidentally, was in sharp disagreement with this endeavor, even to the extent of referring his American sportsmen clients to breeders in Ireland in order for them to have what he obviously considered to be the type of dogs he had originally brought with him to England.

Nonetheless, popular opinion won out, and in 1932 the first Norwich Terrier Club had been formed. We understand that disagreement immediately ensued, primarily centered around color and ear carriage. The

bridge where the stable was located.

Mr. Hopkins originally had crossed a dark brindle Aberdeen-type Scottish Terrier with a longer red Cantab Terrier, the Cantabs being the identification for the strain "Doggy" Lawrence had developed for the Cambridge students. These were said to have combined native small East Anglican Red Terriers (also known as "gypsy dogs" by whom they were thought to have been brought into the area) with Yorkshire and small Irish Terriers.

From this litter came "Rags," who produced a considerable number of offspring due to his being used on many bitches from the area. He was an important influence behind the Jones Terriers, having been used by Mr. Jones on numerous occasions for his bitches in the beginning. Mr. Jones also bought several bitches sired by him.

Ch. Badgewood The Huntress winning the Terrier group under judge and author Anna Katherine Nicholas. Owner, Mrs. Phillip S.P. Fell.

EVOLUTION

EVOLUTION

The Norfolk possesses the true terrier pluck and personality that make him a wonderful addition to any household.

close friend of Sheila Macfie and became a handler for the Colonsays when their owner was ill. The Colonsays were inherited by Alice Hazeldine at the time of Miss Macfie's death. What a splendid tribute to the lady who had invested much time, thought and energy into the recognition of drop-eared Norwich Terriers that her friend Miss Hazeldine piloted one of Sheila Macfie's favorites to become the breed's record-holding Norfolk Terrier, an honor he earned in 1967. This was Ch. Colonsay Orderly Dog, whose retirement found him with 19 Challenge Certificates.

Alice Hazeldine was in charge of another standout drop-ear, Ickworth Ready. Ready had been one puppy in a litter from a breeding at the Kirkby Kennels. He grew up under Alice Hazeldine's ownership and handling to reach an impressive score in Breed and Group wins. But even more notable was his success as a sire.

Drop-eareds and later Norwich Terriers have been exported from England to the United States, Germany, and Sweden.

One of the most familiar names to anyone even remotely interested in the drop-eared Norwich (Norfolk) Terrier is that of the Nanfan Kennels, which has gained an important part in Norfolk history earned by the excellence and success of their dogs. Owned by Joy Taylor, these Norfolks have provided dog shows with some of their most exciting winners. There are at least half a dozen other breeders of whose successful accomplishments we could speak but since this book is just a bare introduction to the breed, it is impossible to cover all of them here.

THE NORFOLK TERRIER AS A PET

An excellent canine character—what better way to describe the Norfolk Terrier? This little dog, despite being small enough to fit in well wherever one may live and being highly adaptable to one's way of life, gives all the pleasures of dog ownership to folks who might never be able to enjoy them were it not for so little a small-sized canine, since many of us for one reason or another are unable to have a big dog or even one of medium size.

If you're looking for a spirited friend with a great sense of humor, the Norfolk is the breed for you! Jaclyn Miller with her two new buddies.

It is a fallacy that small dogs are less fun, or less interesting doggy companions than the large ones. This simply is not true. In fact, there is a steadily increasing number of people discovering that little dogs have much to recommend them, and that in the majority of situations you'll find them every bit as satisfactory to own as a dog six times their size.

NORFOLK TERRIER AS A PET

The Norfolk is a real terrier in every sense of the word, with all of the most loved terrier characteristics. This breed is a true working terrier—hardy, energetic, full of fun, active and dependable—truly a great dog in a small package.

In addition to his proficiency as a working terrier, the Norfolk makes a companion par excellence. With his happy disposition, loyalty and intelligence you will find him a joy to have around. The Norfolk seems almost tireless where children are concerned. They seem to make friends with each other practically on sight and the little Norfolk will be your child's companion and playmate for endless hours. The Norfolk is hardy enough to endure and enjoy the kids, while at the same time being small enough for even a toddler to own.

Norfolks love the companionship of the adults in the family too. They are a handy size to snuggle in your lap or alongside you on the couch while you read or watch television. They are always ready to go for a walk whether in town or in the country and are companionable with other dogs (they seem to have

The Norfolk is a true working terrier—his love of the outdoors and his high energy level are evident to all who meet him. Owner, Mrs. Barbara Miller.

NORFOLK TERRIER AS A PET

His happy disposition and love of his family make the Norfolk Terrier an excellent companion. Max-Well's Witchcraft owned by Mrs. Barbara Miller.

inherited "pack dog tendencies") so they are seldom the ones to start trouble or a fight.

Around your farm or country home, they will take over rodent control promptly and efficiently. After all, was that not the way of life of their ancestors? If you are a sportsman who owns horses and hounds, they will join in the hunt with vigor and efficiency while also being great around the house and stable.

If you are constantly on the move, another asset of the breed is the ease with which you can take him along. A small carrier with him inside can fit very easily under your airplane seat; most hotels or motels have no objection to so small a dog staying in your room (if you do not leave him in the room unattended for hours at a time) and unless your friends are out-and-out dog haters or have a large assortment of pets, few of them will object if you bring one of these little fellows along to visit.

NORFOLK TERRIER AS A PET

Able to fit in anywhere, the adaptable and friendly Norfolk Terrier is the original big dog in a small package.

Their care is simple, too. Small and hardy, they enjoy their food, thrive well on the commercial brands and need just a minimum of coat care or grooming.

For city living, Norfolks should be high on the priority list. Their smallness makes them easy to keep in an apartment. Just pick them up and let them ride in your arms in the elevator; this avoids any objection from people who are afraid of dogs or do not like them, or for any other reason prefer to give them a wide berth. Norfolks are easy to walk on a lead and to pick up after (as city law now demands) due to their size.

And, while this one may surprise you until you think about it, they make marvelous watchdogs, due to their alertness and the speed with which they give voice should anything unexpected occur. Remember, those are the two principal assets of a worthy watchdog. Alertness to notice the unusual and the voice with which to announce the fact will keep strangers with evil intent away with great efficiency. Someone entering premises unlawfully hardly wants a curiously barking dog announcing to the world that an intruder is present and almost invariably will select a more quiet spot in which to work. On the street, too, should anyone approach you in a menacing manner, your Norfolk will proclaim that fact to the world without delay and anyone not wishing to draw a crowd would not linger.

As well as he fares in the city, the Norfolk is basically a country dog; he adapts to the suburbs or the farmlands with ease. He will keep the area rat free, of that you can be sure. If you are a sportsman, he will accompany you and the hounds and the horses,

NORFOLK TERRIER AS A PET

loving every moment of it, making himself useful in the underbrush as he works himself into places far too tight for the hounds to undertake, bolting game, etc.

The Norfolk is an easy dog to train, intelligent and quick. As is the case with any dog, the basic obedience commands should be taught to him if nothing else, particularly for his own safety and your peace of mind. It is essential that a dog understand and obey such commands as "sit" "stay" "come" "down" "heel" and "no." This is very easy with a Norfolk if one starts training when the puppy is two to three months old. Should you encounter any difficulty, then join a training class (your veterinarian or the puppy's breeder can generally tell you how to locate one if this proves a problem). The important thing is that this training not be neglected, as one day your dog's life may depend upon his obeying one of these commands.

The intelligent Norfolk is easy to teach, eager to learn and enjoys the time spent with his owner on training exercises.

ACTIVITIES FOR YOU AND YOUR NORFOLK TERRIER

The ways in that one can enjoy a Norfolk Terrier are several. First is as a family dog, to live with, day in and day out, just having him around with his readily wagging tail and obvious interest in whatever you might like to do. You can enjoy your Norfolk in obedience simply as a well trained family dog, but if you and he truly enjoy working together, there are a series of

NORFOLK TERRIER AS A PET

degrees to be won in competition at obedience trials which can be of great satisfaction.

The first American Norfolk Terrier to win an Obedience degree was Kedrun Dappertutto, CDX, UD, owned by Mary Curtis, who (as a drop-eared Norwich) did so in 1947. Since then at least several dozen little dogs of this breed have gained titular honors by earning degrees.

The Norfolk Terrier is a popular competitor in field trials held by the American Working Terrier Association that are held in all parts of the United States and are open to Dachshunds, Jack Russell Terriers, Glen of Imaal Terriers, and any recognized AKC Terrier Group member able to fit into a nine-inch "earth" hole. There are three classes into which dogs may be entered. The Novice Class, which is for the inexperienced dogs, is divided "A" and "B" for dogs who are

Your Norfolk Terrier will show general interest in whatever activities you want to do. Owner, Mrs. J. Orsi.

under one year old and dogs who have reached that age respectively. When a dog gains a score of 100 in the Novice Class, or is obviously above average in his hunting talents and experience, he is moved up to the Open Class. A dog who has earned the CG (Certificate of Gameness) title may then be entered in the Optional Certificate Class, to compete for the breed's highest score honors.

The first Working Trial Certificate of Merit to be won by a Norfolk (at that time still designated a drop-eared Norwich Terrier) was earned in 1971 by Anne Winston's homebred Ch. Mt. Paul Nanfan.

NORFOLK TERRIER AS A PET

Yarrow's English Muffin owned by Mr. and Mrs. Orville Petty poses on the table for the approval of the judge. Handler, Mary Jane Carberry.

Information regarding the American Working Terrier Association can be obtained by inquiry to the secretary of the American Norfolk Terrier Association, Inc., the name and address of which the American Kennel Club can supply you.

A really fun feature of the Working Terrier Association Trials are the flat races and the hurdle races with which each day's activities usually end—talk about excitement. Even the dogs seem carried away with it as they are urged on by their excited followers.

For those who enjoy showing their Norfolk in conformation competition, it can be a very rewarding and enjoyable hobby, as the breed is an easy one to present nicely for an owner-handler if you are the sort

NORFOLK TERRIER AS A PET

of person who likes getting right in there and doing it yourself. First of all, the dogs are easy to maintain where coat care is concerned; in addition, they are of a size to be manageable with no hassle. These same attributes make them great dogs for the kids to show in Junior Showmanship, too, as even a child can manage them nicely.

One last talent of the Norfolk, of that many may well be unaware, is the breed's distinguishing itself for Hearing Ear work. By their own keen hearing, alertness, and sharp little bark, they can be trained and used for the purposes of alerting people whose hearing is impaired. In other words, they provide ears for the deaf, and as Seeing Eye and guide dogs provide eyes for the blind.

Opposite: Norfolks are great dogs for children to compete with in Junior Showmanship, due to their manageable size and agreeable natures. Dylan Kipp shows her Norfolk to judge Bruce Schwartz.

The Norfolk Terrier has a number of unique qualities that win him friends and admirers wherever he goes!

NORFOLK TERRIER AS A PET

GROOMING YOUR NORFOLK TERRIER

Owners of Norfolk Terriers are fortunate that this breed is among the easiest of the terriers to keep looking his best with a minimum of effort. No extensive grooming procedures are necessary here. The harsh, dense and thick texture of the Norfolk coat makes it highly protective one that resists both dirt and weather. Frequent bathing is not only unnecessary but harmful, as such overuse of shampoo and water will quickly make the coat overly soft.

Even the show coat is a cinch to prepare since emphasis in the breed is placed upon the fact that the dogs should be presented in a *natural* state, and that obvious barbering and shaping should be penalized.

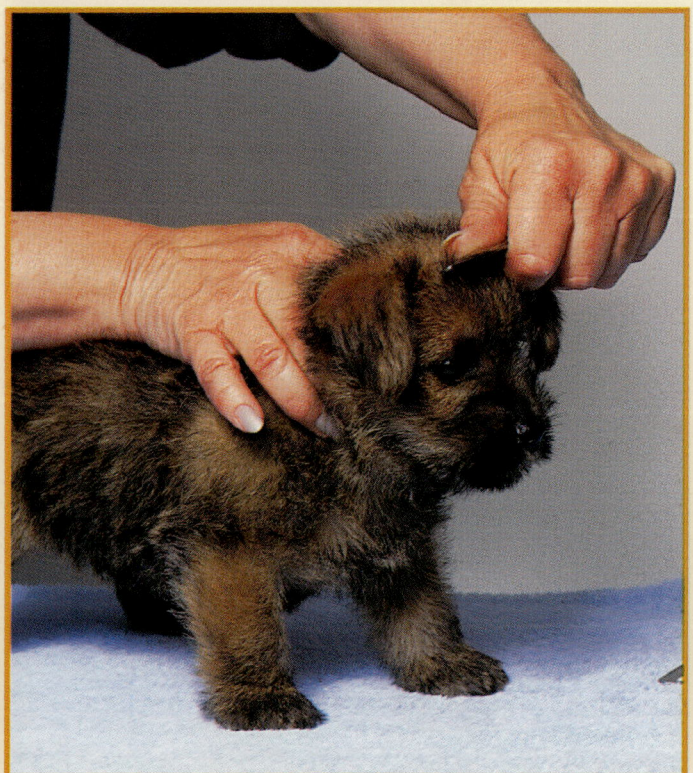

Even as a puppy, your Norfolk should become accustomed to a minimum of grooming. Owner, Mrs. Barbara Miller.

GROOMING

The over-all impression made by a Norfolk should be that of a hardy, business-like, little ratting terrier. He should always give that impression. A good routine for the care of your Norfolk's coat is a daily grooming, plucking out a hair or two here and there if necessary to restore tidiness. Your tools should be, primarily, your thumb and forefinger, a good quality natural bristle brush and a metal comb. By this method, one maintains the coat in a procedure somewhat similar to keeping the grass on your lawn short and dense by frequent mowing. But please do not misun-

When grooming your Norfolk, a metal comb should be used to rake out loose hair.

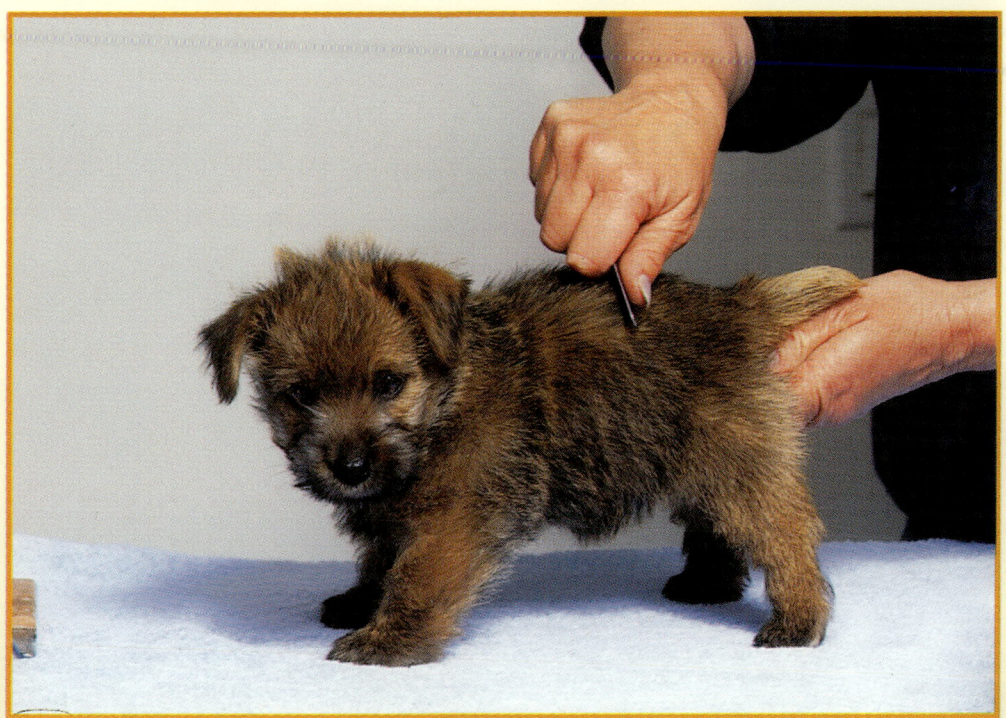

derstand please. By making that comparison I am not suggesting that one should ever "cut down" a Norfolk coat. This is the most disfiguring thing one possibly could do to any member of this breed. The coat should be "plucked" with the fingers or "stripped" with your metal comb but *never* clipped or scissored except, in the latter case, to cut back a scraggly hair (which is better done by fingers) or smooth over around the head or furnishings.

A terrier of any sort whose coat is permitted to just "go wild" soon becomes a real mess and a sad sight indeed. Even as puppies, they should become accustomed to a minimum of grooming (all that will be needed while still so young) to start the youngster off

GROOMING

Even puppies that are a couple of weeks old should have their nails clipped. Snip off the very tip and be careful not to cut the "quick" or vein that runs through the center of the nail.

with a good feeling about having it done. For grooming, it is great to have a rubber-topped grooming table (a necessity if you are planning to exhibit the dog) on which he can feel well grounded. A surface on which the feet will not slip is important, as is having the table stand securely in a position where it is perfectly steady. Place the young Norfolk on the table, petting and talking to him as you do so, then take hold of him gently beneath the chin with your hand and do whatever is necessary for his coat, which will be almost nothing at this stage of the game. The reason for this early "grooming" routine is for the puppy to become aware that the table is perfectly safe and that no dreadful thing will happen to him up there.

Even puppies that are just a couple of weeks old should have their nails clipped. Think of how sharp puppy nails can be and the damage they can inflict on their mother's tender breast area as the pup uses them to hold on when nursing. So as those little needle-like points grow, snip off the very tip. If you start this as an early routine and are careful not to hurt the puppy or make the nails bleed by cutting too much

GROOMING

off the nail tip, going back into the sensitive "quick" (the pinkish strip that runs down the center of the nail), you will help remove the trauma faced by many dogs the moment they even see a pair of nail clippers.

As the puppy approaches four months of age, you will notice the development of loose hair throughout the coat that needs to be removed. For this you need to do a bit of stripping out by the thumb and forefinger method. Working with your wrist rigid, select a few hairs or a small clump at a time, grasp firmly, and pull out. This should be very easy since it is dead hair with which you are working. Starting at the top of the head, work down from side to side until the goal you are interested in achieving has been reached.

Although it is in no way an insurmountable task, neither is the art of plucking terriers an inborn talent. Observation of an expert at work can be extremely helpful; therefore, until you've got it perfected yourself, study exhibitors at work readying their dogs to go into the ring. This is an area in that practice can make

Use a non-skid table when grooming your Norfolk; he will not be able to slip or run away and you will be able to do a thorough job. Owner, Mrs. Barbara Miller.

GROOMING

perfect, so you can expect your expertise to grow as you become more familiar with the technique.

There are two types of coat worn by a Norfolk Terrier. One, the more correct one, is harsh and wiry to the touch; the other softer but longer and more luxuriant, giving the groomer the opportunity to turn out what appears to be a picture of sheer perfection. Bear in mind, though, that the ideal Norfolk coat is harsh, dense and wiry.

Periodically the Norfolk Terrier will "blow" his coat, which translates into "lose the entire coat all at once."

That the time has come is indicated when clumps of fur start hanging out, and the coat takes on a rough uneven appearance, starting to "blow" in clumps. The best way of dealing with this is to get it over with, so start at once to lift out or strip out (with your metal comb, raking the coat firmly) all the hair that is loose. This process will probably need to be repeated several times over a few days, but get it over with as soon as you can in order to clear the way for the fresh, new coat that will start to "make up" immediately.

Remember, *never, ever* use clippers on your Norfolk, or permit anyone else to do so. Taking off the top layer of the coat is not at all what you want done; you need to remove the *entire length* of the hair, not just the top layer. Shearing only the top layer will lead to

Trim the hair on your Norfolk Terrier's paws and inspect his feet as part of his regular grooming regimen.

GROOMING

A well-groomed Norfolk should give the impression of a hardy, business-like little ratting dog. Ch. Paddington's Duke Of Brighton owned by Reggie Higgins and handled by Mary Jane Carberry.

an utterly incorrect texture and make-up of coat, because what you will be doing with the clippers is merely shaving off the outercoat. Don't work with clippers unless you are trying to obtain a soft, unattractive covering on the dog, reminding one of everything undesirable in the Norfolk coat.

The Norfolk is a breed where the ears come in for extra consideration at grooming time, as they are pendulous. Norfolks should be watched for signs of head shaking or undue ear scratching, holding of the head to one side, or vigorous shaking of the head. Should the ear, when you inspect it, have a strong or unpleasant odor, accumulated wax in the ear canal, or any sign of ear mites, clean it out with a cotton swab dipped in peroxide, then apply a suitable ointment into the cavity. If that does not help within a day or two, a trip to the veterinarian is necessary. Do not neglect the ear problems.

Although this is not really a matter of grooming, it seems a likely place to speak of it. The carriage of the Norfolk's ears can go through various changes, especially at times of teething, as the puppy matures. This should settle back to normal in due course, so do not panic if suddenly one ear is carried erect, or in some other deviation from the norm. Chances are this is merely a phase and should settle back when the

GROOMING

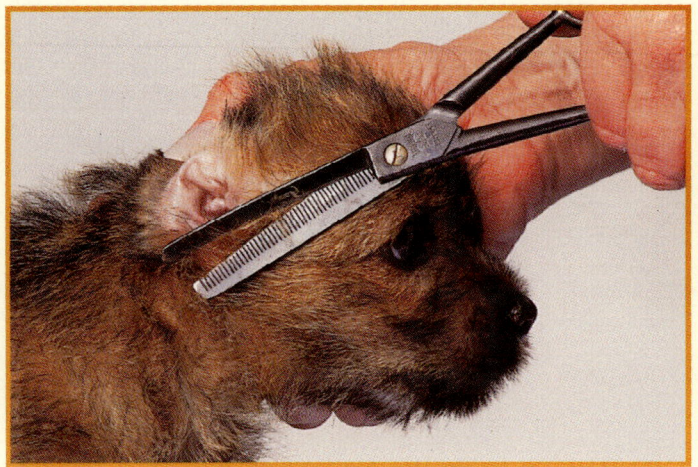

The Norfolk's distinctive drop ears need to be checked regularly for waxy build-up, and the hair around the ear canal must be kept trimmed to prevent infection.

teething time has passed. However, considering the importance of correctly carried ears to the Norfolk's appearance, this being one of the breed's most distinguishing characteristics, do not just sit by and hope for the best. Get busy with some positive action. Additionally, not all puppies are born with the correct pendulous ear carriage of this breed. Some of these, too, may need a bit of assistance to encourage the ears to be carried properly.

The ears, attached as they are to the sides of the head, are expected to and should hang parallel to the cheeks. When the dog is excited, the muscle brings the ear forward; the long edge then resting on the cheek and the blunt tip coming close to the outside corner of the eye.

The Norfolk has an ear of medium size, pliant and expressive. Should one of these ears have a problem in its carriage, such as standing upright, which is one of the phases that can occur, try gently massaging the offender while at the same time encouraging it to remain in the correct position. This may or may not help. If not, there is another course of action; taping up the ear into the correct position. For this procedure, one uses duct tape cut into the shape of a shield that should be trimmed at the corners and attached to the inside of the ear flap, ascertaining that it is holding the ear in the correct position. Holding the ear in place this way for a day or two will often bring it right into line. If it does not, try again, or consult the puppy's breeder for further suggestions. Duct tape is suggested for this purpose as it sticks well, holding firmly, while at the same time it comes off quite easily, causing no pain to the dog.

YOUR PUPPY'S NEW HOME

Before actually collecting your puppy, it is better that you purchase the basic items you will need in advance of the pup's arrival date. This allows you more opportunity to shop around and ensure you have exactly what you want rather than having to buy lesser quality in a hurry.

Make sure both your family and your household are prepared for the arrival of your new Norfolk Terrier puppy. Five-month-old Max-Well's Witch Hunt owned by Barbara Miller.

It is always better to collect the puppy as early in the day as possible. In most instances this will mean that the puppy has a few hours with your family before it is time to retire for his first night's sleep away from his former home.

If the breeder is local, then you may not need any form of box to place the puppy in when you bring him home. A member of the family can hold the pup in his

PUPPY'S NEW HOME

lap—duly protected by some towels just in case the puppy becomes car sick! Be sure to advise the breeder at what time you hope to arrive for the puppy, as this will obviously influence the feeding of the pup that morning or afternoon. If you arrive early in the day, then they will likely only give the pup a light breakfast so as to reduce the risk of travel sickness.

If the trip will be of a few hours duration, you should take a travel crate with you. The crate will provide your pup with a safe place to lie down and rest during the trip. During the trip, the puppy will no doubt wish to relieve his bowels, so you will have to make a few stops. On a long journey you may need a rest yourself, and can take the opportunity to let the puppy get some fresh air. However, do not let the puppy walk where there may have been a lot of other dogs because he

Your Norfolk puppy should be provided with a quiet, comfortable place to rest and relax when he first arrives at his new home.

PUPPY'S NEW HOME

some way soothe him, as the clock ticks to a rhythm not dissimilar from a heart beat. A cuddly toy may also help in the first few weeks. A dim nightlight may provide some comfort to the puppy, because his eyes will not yet be fully able to see in the dark. The puppy may want to leave his bed for a drink or to relieve himself.

If the pup does whimper in the night, there are two things you should not do. One is to get up and chastise him, because he will not understand why you are shouting at him; and the other is to rush to comfort him every time he cries because he will quickly realize that if he wants you to come running all he needs to do is to holler loud enough!

By all means give your puppy some extra attention on his first night, but after this quickly refrain from so doing. The pup will cry for a while but then settle down and go to sleep. Some pups are, of course, worse than others in this respect, so you must use balanced judgment in the matter. Many owners take their pups to bed with them, and there is certainly nothing wrong with this.

The pup will be no trouble in such cases. However, you should only do this if you intend to let this be a permanent arrangement, otherwise it is hardly fair to the puppy. If you have decided to have two puppies,

Provide your Norfolk Terrier with plenty of Nylabones® to keep him out of trouble and to promote constructive chewing.

PUPPY'S NEW HOME

the pup by using your left hand to hold his neck. Now you can lift him and bring him close to your chest. Never lift a pup by his ears and, while he can be lifted by the scruff of his neck where the fur is loose, there is no reason ever to do this, so don't.

Beyond the dangers already cited you may be able to think of other ones that are specific to your home—steep basement steps or the like. Go around your home and check out all potential problems—you'll be glad you did.

THE FIRST NIGHT

The first few nights a puppy spends away from his mother and littermates are quite traumatic for him. He will feel very lonely, maybe cold, and will certainly miss the heartbeat of his siblings when sleeping. To help overcome his loneliness it may help to place a clock next to his bed—one with a loud tick. This will in

Your new Norfolk puppy may miss the company of his dam and littermates when you first bring him home, so try to make him as comfortable as possible. Jacob Miller with a new litter.

43

PUPPY'S NEW HOME

When these Norfolk Terrier puppies are able to leave their mother, their breeder will need to place them with caring, responsible owners.

might pick up an infection. Also, if he relieves his bowels at such a time, do not just leave the feces where they were dropped. This is the height of irresponsibility. It has resulted in many public parks and other places actually banning dogs. You can purchase poop-scoops from your pet shop and should have them with you whenever you are taking the dog out where he might foul a public place.

Your journey home should be made as quickly as possible. If it is a hot day, be sure the car interior is amply supplied with fresh air. It should never be too hot or too cold for the puppy. The pup must never be placed where he might be subject to a draft. If the journey requires an overnight stop at a motel, be aware that other guests will not appreciate a puppy crying half the night. You must regard the puppy as a baby and comfort him so he does not cry for long periods. The worst thing you can do is to shout at or smack him. This will mean your relationship is off to a really bad start. You wouldn't smack a baby, and your puppy is still very much just this.

ON ARRIVING HOME

By the time you arrive home the puppy may be very tired, in which case he should be taken to his

PUPPY'S NEW HOME

Puppies love to chew on things, so make sure that all electrical appliances are neatly hidden from view and unplugged when not in use.

sleeping area and allowed to rest. Children should not be allowed to interfere with the pup when he is sleeping. If the pup is not tired, he can be allowed to investigate his new home—but always under your close supervision. After a short look around, the puppy will no doubt appreciate a light meal and a drink of water. Do not overfeed him at his first meal because he will be in an excited state and more likely to be sick.

Although it is an obvious temptation, you should not invite friends and neighbors around to see the new arrival until he has had at least 48 hours in which to settle down. Indeed, if you can delay this longer then do so, especially if the puppy is not fully vaccinated. At the very least, the visitors might introduce some local bacteria on their clothing that the puppy is not immune to. This aspect is always a risk when a pup has been moved some distance, so the fewer people the pup meets in the first week or so the better.

DANGERS IN THE HOME

Your home holds many potential dangers for a little mischievous puppy, so you must think about these in advance and be sure he is protected from them. The more obvious are as follows:

PUPPY'S NEW HOME

Open Fires. All open fires should be protected by a mesh screen guard so there is no danger of the pup being burned by spitting pieces of coal or wood.

Electrical Wires. Puppies just love chewing on things, so be sure that all electrical appliances are neatly hidden from view and are not left plugged in when not in use. It is not sufficient simply to turn the plug switch to the off position—pull the plug from the socket.

Open Doors. A door would seem a pretty innocuous object, yet with a strong draft it could kill or injure a puppy easily if it is slammed shut. Always ensure

Supervise your Norfolk puppies at all times in the house, especially around the holidays when things like lights, decorations and wrapping paper may be lying around. Owner, Judith Felton.

there is no risk of this happening. It is most likely during warm weather when you have windows or outside doors open and a sudden gust of wind blows through.

Balconies. If you live in a high-rise building, obviously the pup must be protected from falling. Be sure he cannot get through any railings on your patio, balcony, or deck.

Ponds and Pools. A garden pond or a swimming pool is a very dangerous place for a little puppy to be near. Be sure it is well screened so there is no risk of the pup falling in. It takes barely a minute for a pup—or a child—to drown.

The Kitchen. While many puppies will be kept in the kitchen, at least while they are toddlers and not able to control their bowel movements, this is a room full of

41

PUPPY'S NEW HOME

danger—especially while you are cooking. When cooking, keep the puppy in a play pen or in another room where he is safely out of harm's way. Alternatively, if you have a carry box or crate, put him in this so he can still see you but is well protected.

Be aware, when using washing machines, that more than one puppy has clambered in and decided to have a nap and received a wash instead! If you leave the washing machine door open and leave the room for any reason, then be sure to check inside the machine before you close the door and switch on.

Children and Norfolks can be great friends, but make sure you educate your children on the proper way to treat and handle a puppy. Owner, Gregory Siner.

Small Children. Toddlers and small children should never be left unsupervised with puppies. In spite of such advice it is amazing just how many people not only do this but also allow children to pull and maul pups. They should be taught from the outset that a puppy is not a plaything to be dragged about the home—and they should be promptly scolded if they disobey.

Children must be shown how to lift a puppy so it is safe. Failure by you to correctly educate your children about dogs could one day result in their getting a very nasty bite or scratch. When a puppy is lifted, his weight must always be supported. To lift the pup, first place your right hand under his chest. Next, secure

42

PUPPY'S NEW HOME

Be patient and consistent when attempting to housebreak your puppy, as this is one of the first tasks you will undertake together. Owner, Mrs. Barbara Miller.

then they will keep each other company and you will have few problems.

OTHER PETS

If you have other pets in the home then the puppy must be introduced to them under careful supervision. Puppies will get on just fine with any other pets—but you must make due allowance for the respective sizes of the pets concerned, and appreciate that your puppy has a rather playful nature. It would be very foolish to leave him with a young rabbit. The pup will want to play and might bite the bunny and get altogether too rough with it. Kittens are more able to defend themselves from overly cheeky pups, who will get a quick scratch if they overstep the mark. The adult cat could obviously give the pup a very bad scratch, though generally cats will jump clear of pups and watch them from a suitable vantage point. Eventually they will meet at ground level where the cat will quickly hiss and box a puppy's ears. The pup will soon learn to respect an adult cat; thereafter they will probably develop into great friends as the pup matures into an adult dog.

PUPPY'S NEW HOME

HOUSETRAINING

Undoubtedly, the first form of training your puppy will undergo is in respect to his toilet habits. To achieve this you can use either newspaper, or a large litter tray filled with soil or lined with newspaper. A puppy cannot control his bowels until he is a few months old, and not fully until he is an adult. Therefore you must anticipate his needs and be prepared for a few accidents. The prime times a pup will urinate and defecate are shortly after he wakes up from a sleep, shortly after he has eaten, and after he has been playing awhile. He will usually whimper and start searching the

You new Norfolk puppy will look to you, his owner, to take care of all his special needs. Owner, Gregory Siner.

room for a suitable place. You must quickly pick him up and place him on the newspaper or in the litter tray. Hold him in position gently but firmly. He might jump out of the box without doing anything on the first one or two occasions, but if you simply repeat the procedure every time you think he wants to relieve himself then eventually he will get the message.

When he does defecate as required, give him plenty of praise, telling him what a good puppy he is. The litter tray or newspaper must, of course, be cleaned or replaced after each use—puppies do not like using a dirty toilet any more than you do. The pup's toilet can be placed near the kitchen door and as he gets older the tray can be placed outside while the door is open. The pup will then start to use it while

PUPPY'S NEW HOME

he is outside. From that time on, it is easy to get the pup to use a given area of the yard.

Many breeders recommend the popular alternative of crate training. Upon bringing the pup home, introduce him to his crate. The open wire crate is the best choice, placed in a restricted, draft-free area of the home. Put the pup's Nylabone® and other favorite toys in the crate along with a wool blanket or other suitable bedding. The puppy's natural cleanliness instincts prohibit him from soiling in the place where he sleeps, his crate. The puppy should be allowed to go in and out of the open crate during the day, but he should sleep in the crate at the night and at other intervals during the day. Whenever the pup is taken out of his crate, he should be brought outside (or to his newspapers) to do his business. Never use the crate as a place of punishment. You will see how quickly your pup takes to his crate, considering it as his own safe haven from the big world around him.

To properly socialize your Norfolk Terrier puppy, introduce him to as many different people and pets as possible. Owner, Mrs. Barbara Miller.

47

PUPPY'S NEW HOME

THE EARLY DAYS

You will no doubt be given much advice on how to bring up your puppy. This will come from dog-owning friends, neighbors, and through articles and books you may read on the subject. Some of the advice will be sound, some will be nothing short of rubbish. What you should do above all else is to keep an open mind and let common sense prevail over prejudice and worn-out ideas that have been handed down over the centuries. There is no one way that is superior to all others, no more than there is no one dog that is exactly a replica of another. Each is an individual and must always be regarded as such.

A dog never becomes disobedient, unruly, or a menace to society without the full consent of his owner. Your puppy may have many limitations, but the singular biggest limitation he is confronted with in so many instances is his owner's inability to understand his needs and how to cope with them.

IDENTIFICATION

It is a sad reflection on our society that the number of dogs and cats stolen every year runs into many thousands. To these can be added the number that get lost. If you do not want your cherished pet to be lost or stolen, then you should see that he is carrying a permanent identification number, as well as a temporary tag on his collar.

Permanent markings come in the form of tattoos placed either inside the pup's ear flap, or on the inner side of a pup's upper rear leg. The number given is then recorded with one of the national registration companies. Research laboratories will not purchase dogs carrying numbers as they realize these are clearly someone's pet, and not abandoned animals. As a result, thieves will normally abandon dogs so marked and this at least gives the dog a chance to be taken to the police or the dog pound, when the number can be traced and the dog reunited with its family. The only problem with this method at this time is that there are a number of registration bodies, so it is not always apparent which one the dog is registered with (as you provide the actual number). However, each registration body is aware of his competitors and will normally be happy to supply their addresses. Those holding the dog can check out which one you are with. It is not a perfect system, but until such is developed it's the best available.

PUPPY'S NEW HOME

Another permanent form of identification is the microchip, a computer chip that is no bigger than a grain of rice that is injected between the dog's shoulder blades. The dog feels no discomfort. The dog also received a tag that says he is microchipped. If the dog is lost and picked up by the humane society, they can trace the owner by scanning the microchip. It is the safest form of identification.

To keep him from wandering away, make sure your Norfolk is in a fenced-in, secure area when outside.

A temporary tag takes the form of a metal or plastic disk large enough for you to place the dog's name and your phone number on it—maybe even your address as well. In virtually all places you will be required to obtain a license for your puppy. This may not become applicable until the pup is six months old, but it might apply regardless of his age. Much depends upon the state within a country, or the country itself, so check with your veterinarian if the breeder has not already advised you on this.

FEEDING YOUR NORFOLK TERRIER

Dog owners today are fortunate in that they live in an age when considerable cash has been invested in the study of canine nutritional requirements. This means dog food manufacturers are very concerned about ensuring that their foods are of the best quality. The result of all of their studies, apart from the food itself, is that dog owners are bombarded with advertisements telling them why they must purchase a given brand. The number of products available to you is unlimited, so it is hardly surprising to find that dogs in general suffer from obesity and an excess

Norfolk puppies receive their first nutrition from their mothers, but by the time they are ready to go to their new homes they should be on a good-quality, commercial dog food.

of vitamins, rather than the reverse. Be sure to feed age-appropriate food—puppy food up to one year of age, adult food thereafter. Generally breeders recommend dry food supplemented by canned, if needed.

FACTORS AFFECTING NUTRITIONAL NEEDS

Activity Level. A dog that lives in a country environment and is able to exercise for long periods of the day will need more food than the same breed of dog living in an apartment and given little exercise.

FEEDING

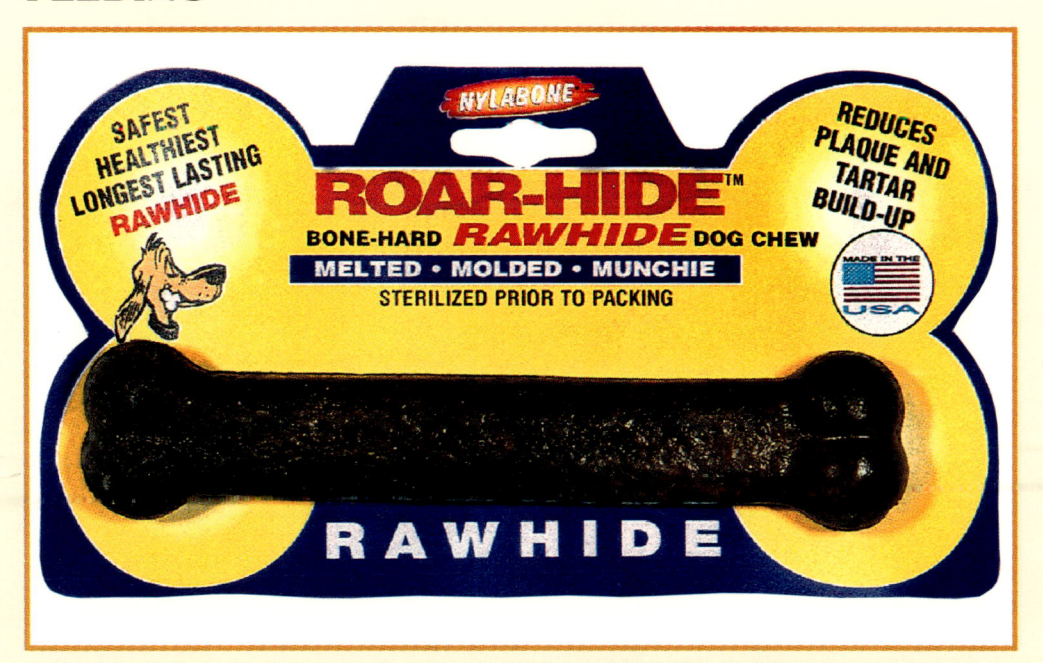

drated. The actual protein content needed in the diet will be determined both by the activity level of the dog and his age. The total protein need will also be influenced by the digestibility factor of the food given.

Fats

These serve numerous roles in the puppy's body. They provide insulation against the cold, and help buffer the organs from knocks and general activity shocks. They provide the richest source of energy, and reserves of this, and they are vital in the transport of vitamins and other nutrients, via the blood, to all other organs. Finally, it is the fat content within a diet that gives it palatability. It is important that the fat content of a diet should not be excessive. This is because the high energy content of fats (more than twice that of protein or carbohydrate) will increase the overall energy content of the diet. The puppy will adjust its food intake to that of its energy needs, which are obviously more easily met in a high-energy diet. This will mean that while the fats are providing the energy needs of the puppy, the overall diet may not be providing its protein, vitamin, and mineral needs, so signs of protein deficiency will become apparent. Rich sources of fats are meat, their byproducts (butter, milk), and vegetable oils, such as safflower, olive, corn or soy bean.

Roar-Hide® is completely edible and is high in protein (over 86%) and low in fat (less than one-third of 1%). Unlike common rawhide, it is safer, less messy, and more fun for your Norfolk.

FEEDING

this process the vitamin content is either greatly reduced or lost altogether. The manufacturer therefore adds vitamins once the heat process has been completed. This is why commercial foods are so useful as part of a feeding regimen, providing they are of good quality and from a company that has prepared the foods very carefully.

Proteins

These are made from amino acids, of which at least ten are essential if a puppy is to maintain healthy growth. Proteins provide the building blocks for the puppy's body. The richest sources are meat, fish and poultry, together with their by-products. The latter will include milk, cheese, yogurt, fishmeal, and eggs. Vegetable matter that has a high protein content includes soy beans, together with numerous corn and other plant extracts that have been dehy-

If you stick to a consistent feeding schedule, your Norfolk will always know when it is feeding time. Owner, Mrs. Barbara Miller.

FEEDING

vitamins and minerals. The other vital ingredient of food is, of course, water. Although all foods obviously contain some of the basic ingredients needed for an animal to survive, they do not all contain the ingredients in the needed ratios or type. For example, there are many forms of protein, just as there are many types of carbohydrates. Both of these compounds are found in meat and in vegetable matter—but not all of those that are needed will be in one particular meat or vegetable. Plants, especially, do not contain certain amino acids that are required for the synthesis of certain proteins needed by dogs.

Likewise, vitamins are found in meats and vegetable matter, but vegetables are a richer source of most. Meat contains very little carbohydrates. Some vitamins can be synthesized by the dog, so do not need to be supplied via the food. Dogs are carnivores and this means their digestive tract has evolved to need a high quantity of meat as compared to humans. The digestive system of carnivores is unable to break down the tough cellulose walls of plant matter, but it is easily able to assimilate proteins from meat.

In order to gain its needed vegetable matter in a form that it can cope with, the carnivore eats all of its prey. This includes the partly digested food within the stomach. In commercially prepared foods, the cellulose is broken down by cooking. During

Carrots are rich in fiber, carbohydrates, and vitamin A. The Carrot Bone™ by Nylabone® is a durable chew containing no plastics or artificial ingredients and it can be served to your Norfolk as-is, in a bone-hard form, or microwaved to a biscuit consistency.

FEEDING

POPpups™ are 100% edible and enhanced with dog-friendly ingredients like liver, cheese, spinach, chicken, carrots, or potatoes. They contain no salt, sugar, alcohol, plastic or preservatives. You can even microwave a POPpup™ to turn into a huge crackly treat for your Norfolk.

Quality of the Food. Obviously the quality of food will affect the quantity required by a puppy. If the nutritional content of a food is low then the puppy will need more of it than if a better quality food was fed.

Balance of Nutrients and Vitamins. Feeding a puppy the correct balance of nutrients is not easy because the average person is not able to measure out ratios of one to another, so it is a case of trying to see that nothing is in excess. However, only tests, or your veterinarian, can be the source of reliable advice.

Genetic and Biological Variation. Apart from all of the other considerations, it should be remembered that each puppy is an individual. His genetic make-up will influence not only his physical characteristics but also his metabolic efficiency. This being so, two pups from the same litter can vary quite a bit in the amount of food they need to perform the same function under the same conditions. If you consider the potential combinations of all of these factors then you will see that pups of a given breed could vary quite a bit in the amount of food they will need. Before discussing feeding quantities it is valuable to know at least a little about the composition of food and its role in the body.

COMPOSITION AND ROLE OF FOOD

The main ingredients of food are protein, fats, and carbohydrates, each of which is needed in relatively large quantities when compared to the other needs of

FEEDING

The puppy should eat his meal in about five to seven minutes. Any leftover food can be discarded or placed into the refrigerator until the next meal (but be sure it is thawed fully if your fridge is very cold).

If the puppy quickly devours its meal and is clearly still hungry, then you are not giving him enough food. If he eats readily but then begins to pick at it, or walks away leaving a quantity, then you are probably giving him too much food. Adjust this at the next meal and you will quickly begin to appreciate what the correct amount is. If, over a number of weeks, the pup starts to look fat, then he is obviously overeating; the reverse is true if he starts to look thin compared with others of the same breed.

WHEN TO FEED

It really does not matter what times of the day the puppy is fed, as long as he receives the needed quantity of food. Puppies from 8 weeks to 12 or 16 weeks need 3 or 4 meals a day. Older puppies and adult dogs should be fed twice a day. What is most important is that the feeding times are reasonably regular. They can be tailored to fit in with your own timetable—for example, 7 a.m. and 6 p.m. The dog will then expect his meals at these times each day. Keeping regular feeding times and feeding set amounts will help you monitor your puppy's or dog's health. If a dog that's normally enthusiastic about mealtimes and eats readily suddenly shows a lack of interest in food, you'll know something's not right.

Choose a good-quality commercial dog food based on your Norfolk's nutritional requirements and his stage in life.

FEEDING

excess can create problems—this applying equally to calcium.

Water

This is the most important of all nutrients, as is easily shown by the fact that the adult dog is made up of about 60 percent water, the puppy containing an even higher percentage. Dogs must retain a water balance, which means that the total intake should be balanced by the total output. The intake comes either by direct input (the tap or its equivalent), plus water released when food is oxidized, known as metabolic water (remember that all foods contain the elements hydrogen and oxygen that recombine in the body to create water). A dog without adequate water will lose condition more rapidly than one depleted of food, a fact common to most animal species.

AMOUNT TO FEED

The best way to determine dietary requirements is by observing the puppy's general health and physical appearance. If he is well covered with flesh, shows good bone development and muscle, and is an active alert puppy, then his diet is fine. A puppy will consume about twice as much as an adult (of the same breed). You should ask the breeder of your puppy to show you the amounts fed to their pups and this will be a good starting point.

The amount you feed your Norfolk will depend on his age and his level of activity.

FEEDING

light, heat, moisture, or rancidity. An excess of vitamins, especially A and D, has been proven to be very harmful. Provided a puppy is receiving a balanced diet, it is most unlikely there will be a deficiency, whereas hypervitaminosis (an excess of vitamins) has become quite common due to owners and breeders feeding unneeded supplements. The only time you should feed extra vitamins to your puppy is if your veterinarian advises you to.

Energetic, growing puppies will need a diet higher in calories than a less active adult. Owner, Mrs. Barbara Miller.

Minerals

These provide strength to bone and cell tissue, as well as assist in many metabolic processes. Examples are calcium, phosphorous, copper, iron, magnesium, selenium, potassium, zinc, and sodium. The recommended amounts of all minerals in the diet has not been fully established. Calcium and phosphorous are known to be important, especially to puppies. They help in forming strong bone. As with vitamins, a mineral deficiency is most unlikely in pups given a good and varied diet. Again, an

FEEDING

Carbohydrates

These are the principal energy compounds given to puppies and adult dogs. Their inclusion within most commercial brand dog foods is for cost, rather than dietary needs. These compounds are more commonly known as sugars, and they are seen in simple or complex compounds of carbon, hydrogen, and oxygen. One of the simple sugars is called glucose, and it is vital to many metabolic processes. When large chains of glucose are created, they form compound sugars. One of these is called glycogen, and it is found in the cells of

If you want to give your Norfolk treats, make sure they are nutritious and do not upset his balanced diet. It looks like this guy is trying to steal the Christmas candy! Owner, Judith Felton.

animals. Another, called starch, is the material that is found in the cells of plants.

Vitamins

These are not foods as such but chemical compounds that assist in all aspects of an animal's life. They help in so many ways that to attempt to describe these effectively would require a chapter in itself. Fruits are a rich source of vitamins, as is the liver of most animals. Many vitamins are unstable and easily destroyed by

TRAINING YOUR NORFOLK TERRIER

Once your puppy has settled into your home and responds to his name, then you can begin his basic training. Before giving advice on how you should go about doing this, two important points should be made. You should train the puppy in isolation of any potential distractions, and you should keep all lessons very short. It is essential that you have the full attention of your puppy. This is not possible if there are other people about, or televisions and radios on, or other pets in the vicinity. Even when the pup has become a young adult, the maximum time you should allocate to a lesson is about 20 minutes. However, you can give the puppy more than one lesson a day, three being as many as are recommended, each well spaced apart.

Before beginning a lesson, always play a little game with the puppy so he is in an active state of mind and thus more receptive to the matter at hand. Like-

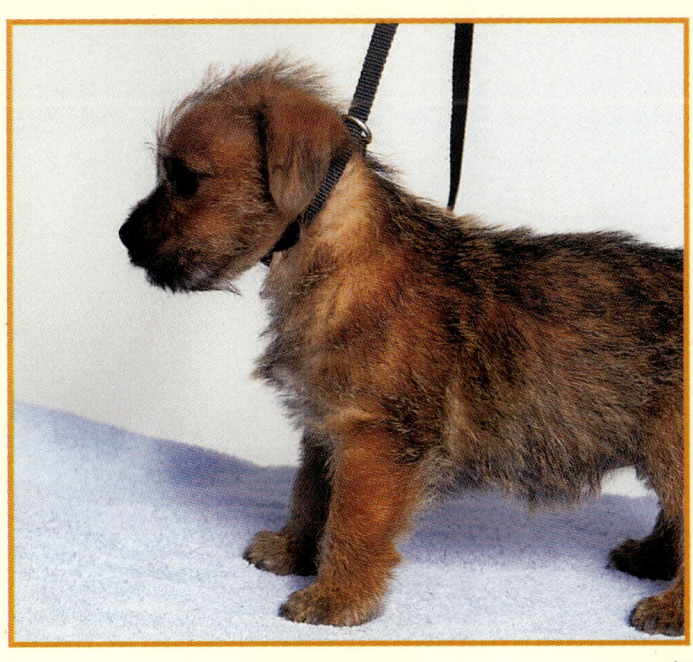

Your Norfolk puppy should learn to walk on a lead not only for his safety but for the safety of others as well. Owner, Mrs. Barbara Miller.

59

TRAINING

wise, always end a lesson with fun-time for the pup, and always—this is most important—end on a high note, praising the puppy. Let the lesson end when the pup has done as you require so he receives lots of fuss. This will really build his confidence.

COLLAR AND LEASH TRAINING

Training a puppy to his collar and leash is very easy. Place a collar on the puppy and, although he will initially try to bite at it, he will soon forget it, the more so if you play with him. You can leave the collar on for a few hours. Some people leave their dogs' collars on all of the time, others only when they are taking the dog out. If it is to be left on, purchase a narrow or round one so it does not mark the fur.

Once the puppy ignores his collar, then you can attach the leash to it and let the puppy pull this along behind it for a few minutes. However, if the pup starts to chew at the leash, simply hold the leash but keep it slack and let the pup go where he wants. The idea is to let him get the feel of the leash, but not get in the habit of chewing it. Repeat this a couple of times a day for two days and the pup will get used to the leash without thinking that it will restrain him—which you will not have attempted to do yet.

Next, you can let the pup understand that the leash will restrict his movements. The first time he realizes this, he will pull and buck or just sit down. Immediately call the pup to you and give him lots of fuss. Never tug on the leash so the puppy is dragged along the floor, as this simply implants a negative thought in his mind.

THE COME COMMAND

Come is the most vital of all commands and especially so for the independently minded dog. To teach the puppy to come, let him reach the end of a long lead, then give the command and his name, gently pulling him toward you at the same time. As soon as he associates the word come with the action of moving toward you, pull only when he does not respond immediately. As he starts to come, move back to make him learn that he must come from a distance as well as when he is close to you. Soon you may be able to practice without a leash, but if he is slow to come or notably disobedient, go to him and

TRAINING

pull him toward you, repeating the command. Never scold a dog during this exercise—or any other exercise. Remember the trick is that the puppy must want to come to you. For the very independent dog, hand signals may work better than verbal commands.

THE SIT COMMAND

As with most basic commands, your puppy will learn this one in just a few lessons. You can give the puppy two lessons a day on the sit command but he will make just as much progress with one 15-minute lesson each day. Some trainers will advise you that you should not proceed to other commands until the previous one has been learned really well. However, a bright young pup is quite capable of handling more than one command per lesson, and certainly per day. Indeed, as time progresses, you will be going through each command as a matter of routine before a new

With proper training, who knows how far you Norfolk can go? Handler Mary Jane Carberry gaits Yarrow's English Muffin around the show ring.

TRAINING

one is attempted. This is so the puppy always starts, as well as ends, a lesson on a high note, having successfully completed something.

Call the puppy to you and fuss over him. Place one hand on his hindquarters and the other under his upper chest. Say "Sit" in a pleasant (never harsh) voice. At the same time, push down his rear end and push up under his chest. Now lavish praise on the puppy. Repeat this a few times and your pet will get the idea. Once the puppy is in the sit position you will release your hands. At first he will tend to get up, so immediately repeat the exercise. The lesson will end when the pup is in the sit position. When the puppy understands the command, and does it right away, you can slowly move backwards so that you are a few feet away from him. If he attempts to come to you, simply place him back in the original position and start again. Do not attempt to keep the pup in the sit position for too long. At this age, even a few seconds is a long while and you do not want him to get bored with lessons before he has even begun them.

THE HEEL COMMAND

All dogs should be able to walk nicely on a leash without their owners being involved in a tug-of-war. The heel command will follow leash training. Heel training is best done where you have a wall to one side of you. This will restrict the puppy's lateral movements, so you only have to contend with forward and backward situations. A fence is an alternative, or you can do the lesson in the garage. Again, it is better to do the lesson in private, not on a public sidewalk where there will be many distractions.

With a puppy, there will be no need to use a choke collar as you can be just as effective with a regular one. The leash should be of good length, certainly not too short. You can adjust the space between you, the puppy, and the wall so your pet has only a small amount of room to move sideways. This being so, he will either hang back or pull ahead—the latter is the more desirable state as it indicates a bold pup who is not frightened of you.

Hold the leash in your right hand and pass it through your left. As the puppy moves ahead and strains on the leash, give the leash a quick jerk backwards with your left hand, at the same time saying "Heel." The position you want the pup to be in is such that his chest

TRAINING

A well-mannered Norfolk Terrier is a pleasure to own and will be welcomed anywhere.

is level with, or just behind, an imaginary line from your knee. When the puppy is in this position, praise him and begin walking again, and the whole exercise will be repeated. Once the puppy begins to get the message, you can use your left hand to pat the side of your knee so the pup is encouraged to keep close to your side.

It is useful to suddenly do an about-turn when the pup understands the basics. The puppy will now be behind you, so you can pat your knee and say "Heel." As soon as the pup is in the correct position, give him lots of praise. The puppy will now be beginning to associate certain words with certain actions. Whenever he is not in the heel position he will experience displeasure as you jerk the leash, but when he comes alongside you he will receive praise. Given these two options, he will always prefer the latter—assuming he has no other reason to fear you, which would then create a dilemma in his mind.

Once the lesson has been well learned, then you can adjust your pace from a slow walk to a quick one and the puppy will come to adjust. The slow walk is always the more difficult for most puppies, as they are usually anxious to be on the move.

If you have no wall to walk against then things will be a little more difficult because the pup will tend to wander to his left. This means you need to give lateral

63

TRAINING

jerks as well as bring the pup to your side. End the lesson when the pup is walking nicely beside you. Begin the lesson with a few sit commands (which he understands by now), so you're starting with success and praise. If your puppy is nervous on the leash, you should never drag him to your side as you may see so many other people do (who obviously didn't invest in a good book like you did!). If the pup sits down, call him to your side and give lots of praise. The pup must always come to you because he wants to. If he is dragged to your side he will see you doing the dragging—a big negative. When he races ahead he does not see you jerk the leash, so all he knows is that something restricted his movement and, once he was in a given position, you gave him lots of praise. This is using canine psychology to your advantage.

Always try to remember that if a dog must be disciplined, then try not to let him associate the discipline with you. This is not possible in all matters but, where it is, this is definitely to be preferred.

THE STAY COMMAND

This command follows from the sit. Face the puppy and say "Sit." Now step backwards, and as you do, say "Stay." Let the pup remain in the position for only a few seconds before calling him to you and giving lots of praise. Repeat this, but step further back. You do not need to shout at the puppy. Your pet is not deaf; in fact, his hearing is far better than yours. Speak just loudly enough for the pup to hear, yet use a firm voice. You can stretch the word to form a "sta-a-a-y." If the pup gets up and comes to you simply lift him up, place him back in the original position, and start again. As the pup comes to understand the command, you can move further and further back.

The next test is to walk away after placing the pup. This will mean your back is to him, which will tempt him to follow you. Keep an eye over your shoulder, and the minute the pup starts to move, spin around and, using a sterner voice, say either "Sit" or "Stay." If the pup has gotten quite close to you, then, again, return him to the original position.

As the weeks go by you can increase the length of time the pup is left in the stay position—but two to three minutes is quite long enough for a puppy. If your puppy drops into a lying position and is clearly more comfortable, there is nothing wrong with this. Like-

TRAINING

wise, your pup will want to face the direction in which you walked off. Some trainers will insist that the dog faces the direction he was placed in, regardless of whether you move off on his blind side. I have never believed in this sort of obedience because it has no practical benefit.

THE DOWN COMMAND

From the puppy's viewpoint, the down command can be one of the more difficult ones to accept. This

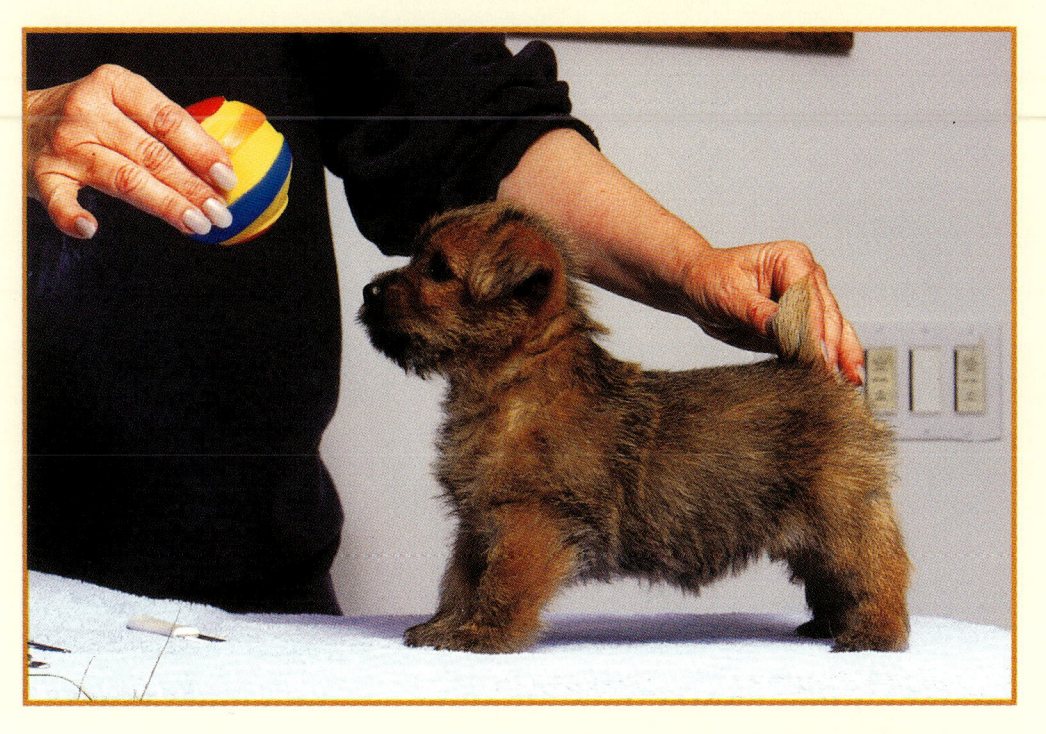

The time you spend with your puppy practicing training exercises will result in a close bond between you and your Norfolk.

is because the position is one taken up by a submissive dog in a wild pack situation. A timid dog will roll over—a natural gesture of submission. A bolder pup will want to get up, and might back off, not feeling he should have to submit to this command. He will feel that he is under attack from you and about to be punished—which is what would be the position in his natural environment. Once he comes to understand this is not the case, he will accept this unnatural position without any problem.

You may notice that some dogs will sit very quickly, but will respond to the down command more slowly—it is their way of saying that they will obey the command, but under protest!

There two ways to teach this command. One is, in my mind, more intimidating than the other, but it is up

TRAINING

to you to decide which one works best for you. The first method is to stand in front of your puppy and bring him to the sit position, with his collar and leash on. Pass the leash under your left foot so that when you pull on it, the result is that the pup's neck is forced downwards. With your free left hand, push the pup's shoulders down while at the same time saying "Down." This is when a bold pup will instantly try to back off and wriggle in full protest. Hold the pup firmly by the shoulders so he stays in the position for a second or two, then tell him what a good dog he is and give him lots of praise. Repeat this only a few times in a lesson because otherwise the puppy will get bored and upset over this command. End with an easy command that brings back the pup's confidence.

The second method, and the one I prefer, is done as follows: Stand in front of the pup and then tell him to sit. Now kneel down, which is immediately far less intimidating to the puppy than to have you towering above him. Take each of his front legs and pull them forward, at the same time saying "Down." Release the legs and quickly apply light pressure on the shoulders with your left hand. Then, as quickly, say "Good boy" and give lots of fuss. Repeat two or three times only. The pup will learn over a few lessons. Remember, this is a very submissive act on the pup's behalf, so there is no need to rush matters.

RECALL TO HEEL COMMAND

When your puppy is coming to the heel position from an off-leash situation—such as if he has been running free—he should do this in the correct manner. He should pass behind you and take up his position and then sit. To teach this command, have the pup in front of you in the sit position with his collar and leash on. Hold the leash in your right hand. Give him the command to heel, and pat your left knee. As the pup starts to move forward, use your right hand to guide him behind you. If need be you can hold his collar and walk the dog around the back of you to the desired position. You will need to repeat this a few times until the dog understands what is wanted.

When he has done this a number of times, you can try it without the collar and leash. If the pup comes up toward your left side, then bring him to the sit position in front of you, hold his collar and walk him around the back of you. He will eventually understand and automatically pass around your back each time. If the dog

TRAINING

is already behind you when you recall him, then he should automatically come to your left side, which you will be patting with your hand.

THE NO COMMAND

This is a command that must be obeyed every time without fail. There are no halfway stages, he must be 100-percent reliable. Most delinquent dogs have never been taught this command; included in these are the jumpers, the barkers, and the biters. Were your puppy to approach a poisonous snake or any other potential danger, the no command, coupled with the recall, could save his life. You do not need to give a specific lesson for this command because it will crop up time and again in day-to-day life.

If the puppy is chewing a slipper, you should approach the pup, take hold of the slipper, and say "No" in a stern voice. If he jumps onto the furniture, lift him off and say "No" and place him gently on the floor. You must be consistent in the use of the command and apply it every time he is doing something you do not want him to do.

A family affair! The Kipp family with Best in Show winner Ch. Max-Well's Weatherman.

YOUR HEALTHY NORFOLK TERRIER

Dogs, like all other animals, are capable of contracting problems and diseases that, in most cases, are easily avoided by sound husbandry—meaning well-bred and well-cared-for animals are less prone to developing diseases and problems than are carelessly bred and neglected animals. Your knowledge of how to avoid problems is far more valuable than all of the books and advice on how to cure them. Respectively, the only person you should listen to about treatment is your vet. Veterinarians don't have all the answers, but at least they are trained to analyze and treat illnesses, and are aware of the full implications of treatments. This does not mean a few old remedies aren't good standbys when all else fails, but in most cases modern science provides the best treatments for disease.

Opposite: A thorough oral exam should be part of your Norfolk Terrier's regular check-up.

PHYSICAL EXAMS

Your puppy should receive regular physical examinations or check-ups. These come in two forms. One is obviously performed by your vet, and the other is a day-to-day procedure that should be done by you. Apart from the fact the exam will highlight any problem at an early stage, it is an excellent way of socializing the pup to being handled.

To do the physical exam yourself, start at the head and work your way around the body. You are looking for any sign of lesions, or any indication of parasites on the pup. The most common parasites are fleas and ticks.

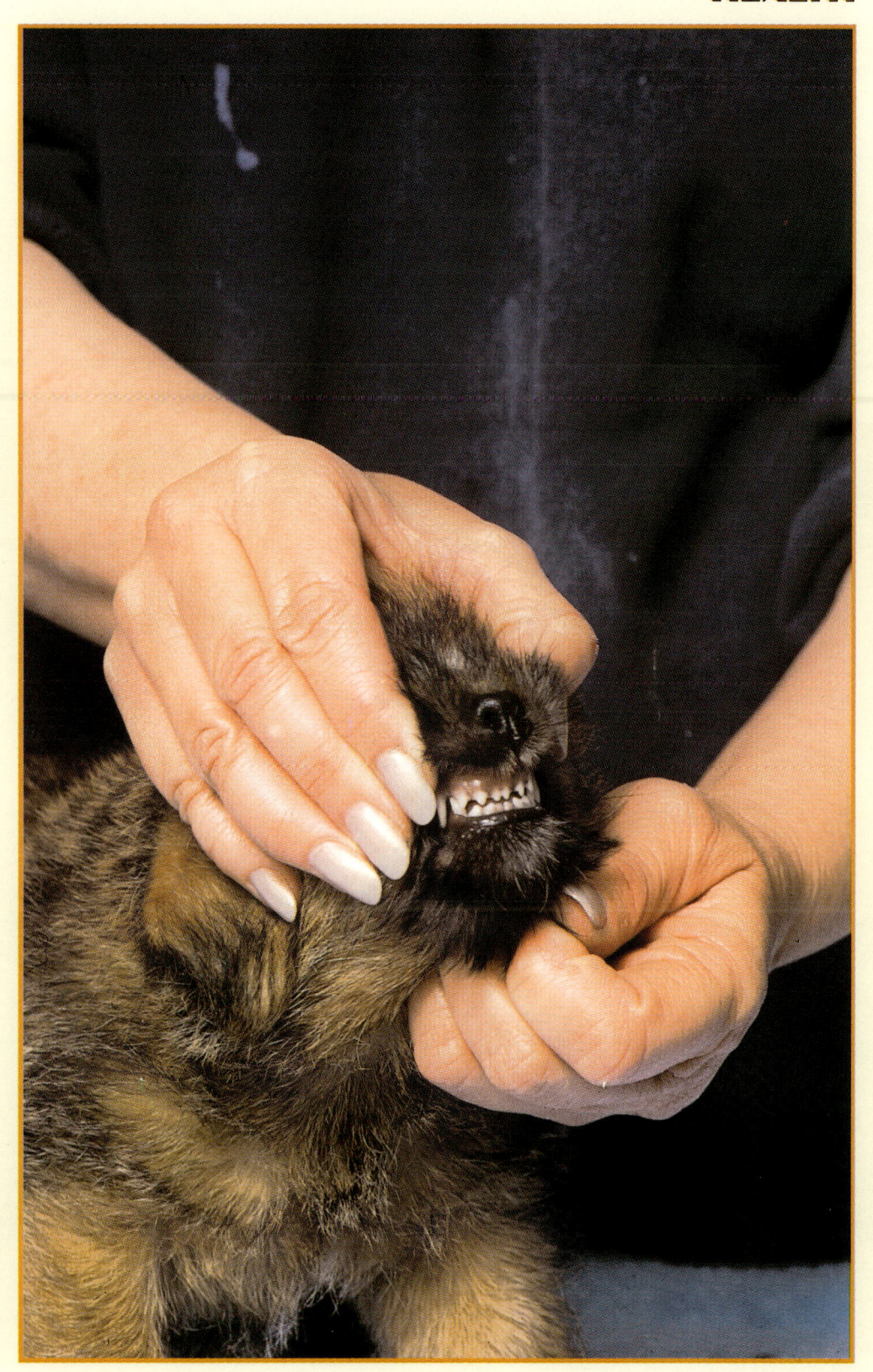

HEALTH

HEALTH

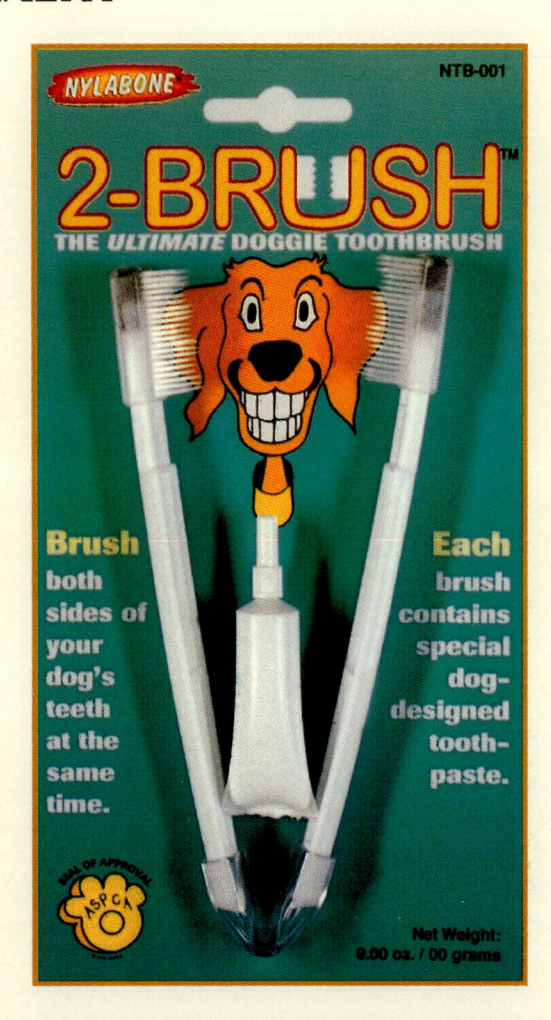

2-Brush™ is made with two toothbrushes to clean both sides of your Norfolk's teeth at the same time, and each brush contains a toothpaste reservoir designed to apply the toothpaste, which is specially formulated for dogs, directly into the brush.

HEALTHY TEETH AND GUMS

Chewing is instinctual. Puppies chew so that their teeth and jaws grow strong and healthy as they develop. As the permanent teeth begin to emerge, it is painful and annoying to the puppy, and puppy owners must recognize that their new charges need something safe upon which to chew. Unfortunately, once the puppy's permanent teeth have emerged and settled solidly into the jaw, the chewing instinct does not fade. Adult dogs instinctively need to clean their teeth, massage their gums, and exercise their jaws through chewing.

It is necessary for your dog to have clean teeth. You should take your dog to the veterinarian at least once a year to have his teeth cleaned and to have his mouth examined for any sign of oral disease. Although dogs do not get cavities in the same way humans do, dogs'

HEALTH

The Hercules® by Nylabone® has raised dental tips that help fight plaque on your Norfolk Terrier's teeth and gums.

teeth accumulate tartar, and more quickly than humans do! Veterinarians recommend brushing your dog's teeth daily. But who can find time to brush their dog's teeth daily? The accumulation of tartar and plaque on our dog's teeth when not removed can cause irritation and eventually erode the enamel and finally destroy the teeth. Advanced cases, while destroying the teeth, bring on gingivitis and periodontitis, two very serious conditions that can affect the dog's internal organs as well...to say nothing about bad breath!

Since everyone can't brush their dog's teeth daily or get to the veterinarian often enough for him to scale

Nylafloss® does wonders for your Norfolk Terrier's dental health by massaging his gums and literally flossing between his teeth, loosening plaque and tartar build-up. Unlike cotton tug toys, Nylafloss® won't rot or fray.

71

HEALTH

the dog's teeth, providing the dog with something safe to chew on will help maintain oral hygeine. Chew devices from Nylabone® keep dogs' teeth clean, but they also provide an excellent resource for entertainment and relief of doggie tensions. Nylabone® products give your dog something to do for an hour or two every day and during that hour or two, your dog will be taking an active part in keeping his teeth and gums healthy…without even realizing it! That's invaluable to your dog, and valuable to you!

Nylabone® provides fun bones, challenging bones, and *safe* bones. It is an owner's responsibility to recognize safe chew toys from dangerous ones. Your dog will chew and devour anything you give him. Dogs must not be permitted to chew on items that they can break. Pieces of broken objects can do internal damage to a dog, besides ripping the dog's mouth. Cheap plastic or rubber toys can cause stoppage in the intestines; such stoppages are operable only if caught immediately.

The most obvious choices, in this case, may be the worst choice. Natural beef bones were not designed for chewing and cannot take too much pressure from the sides. Due to the abrasive nature of these bones, they should be offered most sparingly. Knuckle bones, though once very popular for dogs, can be easily

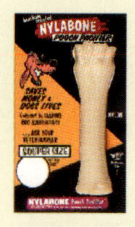

Nylabone® is the only plastic dog bone made of 100% virgin nylon, specially processed to create a tough, durable, completely safe bone.

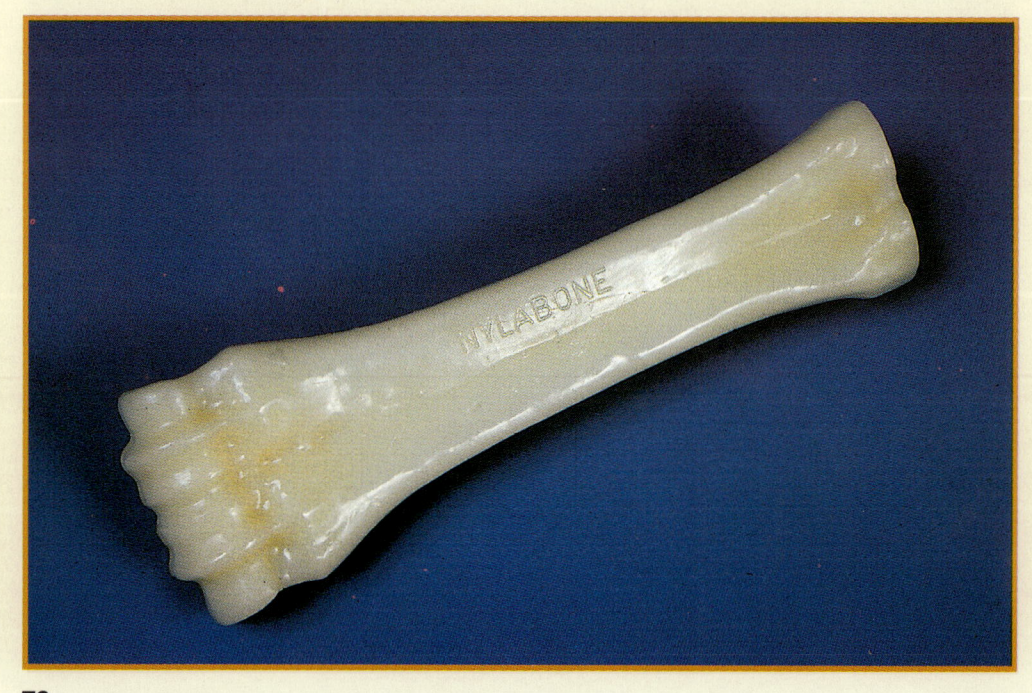

HEALTH

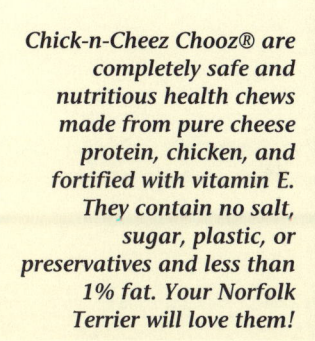

Chick-n-Cheez Chooz® are completely safe and nutritious health chews made from pure cheese protein, chicken, and fortified with vitamin E. They contain no salt, sugar, plastic, or preservatives and less than 1% fat. Your Norfolk Terrier will love them!

chewed up and eaten by dogs. At the very least, digestion is interrupted; at worst, the dog can choke or suffer from intestinal blockage.

When a dog chews hard on a Nylabone®, little bristle-like projections appear on the surface of the bone. These help to clean the dog's teeth and add to the gum-massaging. Given the chemistry of the nylon, the bristle can pass through the dog's intestinal tract without effect. Since nylon is inert, no microorganism can grow on it, and it can be washed in soap and water or sterilized in boiling water or in an autoclave.

For the sake of your dog, his teeth and your own peace of mind, provide your dog with Nylabones®. They have 100 variations from which to choose.

FIGHTING FLEAS

Fleas are very mobile and may be red, black, or brown in color. The adults suck the blood of the host, while the larvae feed on the feces of the adults, which is rich in blood. Flea "dirt" may be seen on the pup as very tiny clusters of blackish specks that look like freshly ground pepper. The eggs of fleas may be laid

HEALTH

on the puppy, though they are more commonly laid off the host in a favorable place, such as the bedding. They normally hatch in 4 to 21 days, depending on the temperature, but they can survive for up to 18 months if temperature conditions are not favorable. The larvae are maggot-like and molt a couple of times before forming pupae, which can survive long periods until the temperature, or the vibration of a nearby host, causes them to emerge and jump on a host.

There are a number of effective treatments available, and you should discuss them with your veterinarian, then follow all instructions for the one you choose. Any treatment will involve a product for your puppy or dog and one for the environment, and will require diligence on your part to treat all areas and thoroughly clean your home and yard until the infestation is eradicated.

THE TROUBLE WITH TICKS

Ticks are arthropods of the spider family, which means they have eight legs (though the larvae have six). They bury their headparts into the host and gorge on its blood. They are easily seen as small grain-like creatures sticking out from the skin. They are often picked up when dogs play in fields, but may also arrive in your yard via wild animals—even birds—or stray cats and dogs. Some ticks are species-specific, others are more adaptable and will host on many species.

The cat flea is the most common flea of dogs. It starts feeding soon after it makes contact with the dog.

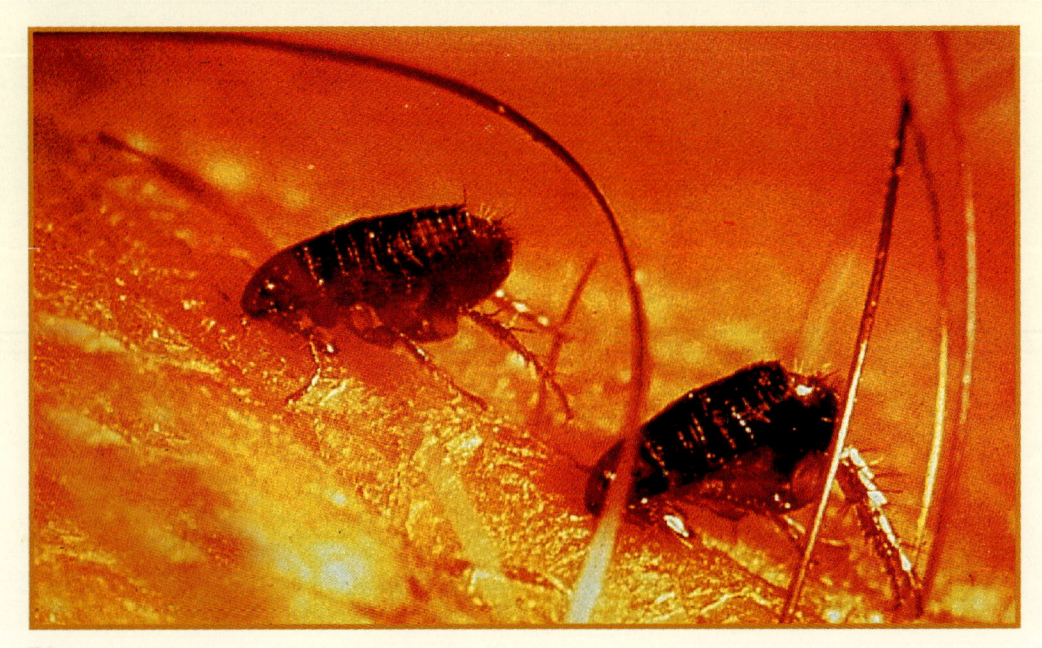

HEALTH

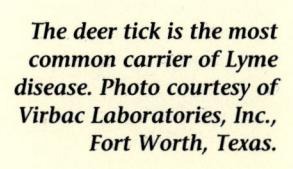

The deer tick is the most common carrier of Lyme disease. Photo courtesy of Virbac Laboratories, Inc., Fort Worth, Texas.

The most troublesome type of tick is the deer tick, which spreads the deadly Lyme disease that can cripple a dog (or a person). Deer ticks are tiny and very hard to detect. Often, by the time they're big enough to notice, they've been feeding on the dog for a few days—long enough to do their damage. Lyme disease was named for the area of the United States in which it was first detected—Lyme, Connecticut—but has now been diagnosed in almost all parts of the U.S. Your veterinarian can advise you of the danger to your dog(s) in your area, and may suggest your dog be vaccinated for Lyme. Always go over your dog with a fine-toothed flea comb when you come in from walking through any area that may harbor deer ticks, and if your dog is acting unusually sluggish or sore, seek veterinary advice.

Attempts to pull a tick free will invariably leave the headpart in the pup, where it will die and cause an infected wound or abscess. The best way to remove ticks is to dab a strong saline solution, iodine, or alcohol on them. This will numb them, causing them to loosen their hold, at which time they can be removed with forceps. The wound can then be cleaned and covered with an antiseptic ointment. If ticks are common in your area, consult with your vet for a suitable pesticide to be used in kennels, on bedding, and on the puppy or dog.

INSECTS AND OTHER OUTDOOR DANGERS

There are many biting insects, such as mosquitoes, that can cause discomfort to a puppy. Many

HEALTH

diseases are transmitted by the males of these species.

A pup can easily get a grass seed or thorn lodged between his pads or in the folds of his ears. These may go unnoticed until an abscess forms.

This is where your daily check of the puppy or dog will do a world of good. If your puppy has been playing in long grass or places where there may be thorns, pine needles, wild animals, or parasites, the check-up is a wise precaution.

SKIN DISORDERS

Apart from problems associated with lesions created by biting pests, a puppy may fall foul to a number of other skin disorders. Examples are ringworm, mange, and eczema. Ringworm is not caused by a worm, but is a fungal infection. It manifests itself as a sore-looking bald circle. If your puppy should have any form of bald patches, let your veterinarian check him over; a microscopic examination can confirm the condition. Many old remedies for ringworm exist, such as iodine, carbolic acid, formalin, and other tinctures, but modern drugs are superior.

Your Norfolk can pick up parasites like fleas and ticks when outside. Make sure your check your dog's coat thoroughly after playing outdoors.

HEALTH

Fungal infections can be very difficult to treat, and even more difficult to eradicate, because of the spores. These can withstand most treatments, other than burning, which is the best thing to do with bedding once the condition has been confirmed.

Mange is a general term that can be applied to many skin conditions where the hair falls out and a flaky crust develops and falls away.

Often, dogs will scratch themselves, and this invariably is worse than the original condition, for it opens lesions that are then subject to viral, fungal, or parasitic attack. The cause of the problem can be various species of mites. These either live on skin debris and the hair follicles, which they destroy, or they bury themselves just beneath the skin and feed on the tissue. Applying general remedies from pet stores is not recommended because it is essential to identify the type of mange before a specific treatment is effective.

Eczema is another non-specific term applied to many skin disorders. The condition can be brought about in many ways. Sunburn, chemicals, allergies to foods, drugs, pollens, and even stress can all produce a deterioration of the skin and coat. Given the range of causal factors, treatment can be difficult because the problem is one of identification. It is a case of taking each possibility at a time and trying to correctly diagnose the matter. If the cause is of a dietary nature then you must remove one item at a time in order to find out if the dog is allergic to a given food. It could, of course, be the lack of a nutrient that is the problem, so if the condition persists, you should consult your veterinarian.

INTERNAL DISORDERS

It cannot be overstressed that it is very foolish to attempt to diagnose an internal disorder without the advice of a veterinarian. Take a relatively common problem such as diarrhea. It might be caused by nothing more serious than the puppy hogging a lot of food or eating something that it has never previously eaten. Conversely, it could be the first indication of a potentially fatal disease. It's up to your veterinarian to make the correct diagnosis.

The following symptoms, especially if they accompany each other or are progressively added to earlier symptoms, mean you should visit the veterinarian right away:

HEALTH

Continual vomiting. All dogs vomit from time to time and this is not necessarily a sign of illness. They will eat grass to induce vomiting. It is a natural cleansing process common to many carnivores. However, continued vomiting is a clear sign of a problem. It may be a blockage in the pup's intestinal tract, it may be induced by worms, or it could be due to any number of diseases.

Diarrhea. This, too, may be nothing more than a temporary condition due to many factors. Even a change of home can induce diarrhea, because this often stresses the pup, and invariably there is some change in the diet. If it persists more than 48 hours then something is amiss. If blood is seen in the feces, waste no time at all in taking the dog to the vet.

Running eyes and/or nose. A pup might have a chill and this will cause the eyes and nose to weep. Again, this should quickly clear up if the puppy is placed in a warm environment and away from any drafts. If it does not, and especially if a mucous discharge is seen, then the pup has an illness that must be diagnosed.

Coughing. Prolonged coughing is a sign of a problem, usually of a respiratory nature.

Wheezing. If the pup has difficulty breathing and makes a wheezing sound when breathing, then something is wrong.

Cries when attempting to defecate or urinate. This might only be a minor problem due to the hard state of the feces, but it could be more serious, especially if the pup cries when urinating.

Cries when touched. Obviously, if you do not handle a puppy with care he might yelp. However, if he cries even when lifted gently, then he has an internal problem that becomes apparent when pressure is applied to a given area of the body. Clearly, this must be diagnosed.

Refuses food. Generally, puppies and dogs are greedy creatures when it comes to feeding time. Some might be more fussy, but none should refuse more than one meal. If they go for a number of hours without showing any interest in their food, then something is not as it should be.

General listlessness. All puppies have their off days when they do not seem their usual cheeky, mischievous selves. If this condition persists for more than two days then there is little doubt of a problem. They may not show any of the signs listed, other than

HEALTH

perhaps a reduced interest in their food. There are many diseases that can develop internally without displaying obvious clinical signs. Blood, fecal, and other tests are needed in order to identify the disorder before it reaches an advanced state that may not be treatable.

WORMS

There are many species of worms, and a number of these live in the tissues of dogs and most other animals. Many create no problem at all, so you are not even aware they exist. Others can be tolerated in small levels, but become a major problem if they number more than a few. The most common types seen in dogs are roundworms and tapeworms. While roundworms are the greater problem, tapeworms require an intermediate host so are more easily eradicated.

Roundworms are spaghetti-like worms that cause a pot-bellied appearance and dull coat, along with more severe symptoms, such as diarrhea and vomiting. Photo courtesy of Merck AgVet.

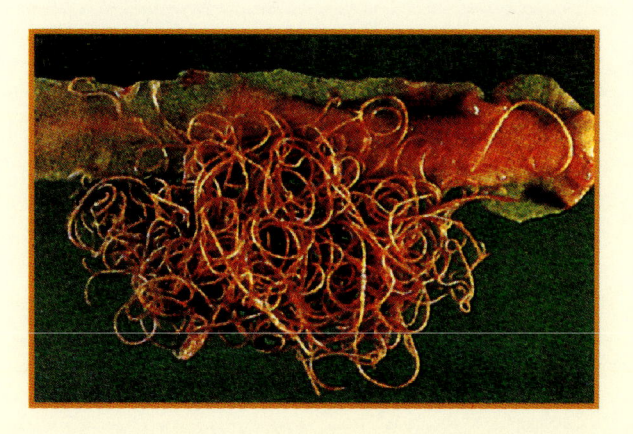

Roundworms of the species *Toxocara canis* infest the dog. They may grow to a length of 8 inches (20 cm) and look like strings of spaghetti. The worms feed on the digesting food in the pup's intestines. In chronic cases the puppy will become pot-bellied, have diarrhea, and will vomit. Eventually, he will stop eating, having passed through the stage when he always seems hungry. The worms lay eggs in the puppy and these pass out in his feces. They are then either ingested by the pup, or they are eaten by mice, rats, or beetles. These may then be eaten by the puppy and the life cycle is complete.

Larval worms can migrate to the womb of a pregnant bitch, or to her mammary glands, and this is how they pass to the puppy. The pregnant bitch can be wormed, which will help. The pups can, and should,

HEALTH

Whipworms are hard to find unless you strain your dog's feces, and this is best left to a veterinarian. Pictured here are adult whipworms.

be wormed when they are about two weeks old. Repeat worming every 10 to 14 days and the parasites should be removed. Worms can be extremely dangerous to young puppies, so you should be sure the pup is wormed as a matter of routine.

Tapeworms can be seen as tiny rice-like eggs sticking to the puppy's or dog's anus. They are less destructive, but still undesirable. The eggs are eaten by mice, fleas, rabbits, and other animals that serve as intermediate hosts. They develop into a larval stage and the host must be eaten by the dog in order to complete the chain. Your vet will supply a suitable remedy if tapeworms are seen or suspected. There are other worms, such as hookworms and whipworms, that are also blood suckers. They will make a pup anemic, and blood might be seen in the feces, which can be examined by the vet to confirm their presence. Cleanliness in all matters is the best preventative measure for all worms.

Heartworm infestation in dogs is passed by mosquitoes but can be prevented by a monthly (or daily) treatment that is given orally. Talk to your vet about the risk of heartworm in your area.

BLOAT (GASTRIC DILATATION)

This condition has proved fatal in many dogs, especially large and deep-chested breeds, such as the Weimaraner and the Great Dane. However, any dog can get bloat. It is caused by swallowing air during exercise, food/water gulping or another strenuous task. As many believe, it is not the result of flatulence. The stomach of an affected dog twists, disallowing

HEALTH

food and blood flow and resulting in harmful toxins being released into the bloodstream. Death can easily follow if the condition goes undetected.

The best preventative measure is not to feed large meals or exercise your puppy or dog immediately after he has eaten. Veterinarians recommend feeding three smaller meals per day in an elevated feeding rack, adding water to dry food to prevent gulping, and not offering water during mealtimes.

VACCINATIONS

Every puppy, purebred or mixed breed, should be vaccinated against the major canine diseases. These are distemper, leptospirosis, hepatitis, and canine parvovirus. Your puppy may have received a temporary vaccination against distemper before you purchased him, but be sure to ask the breeder to be sure.

The age at which vaccinations are given can vary, but will usually be when the pup is 8 to 12 weeks old. By this time any protection given to the pup by antibodies received from his mother via her initial milk feeds will be losing their strength.

The puppy's immune system works on the basis that the white blood cells engulf and render harmless

Rely on your veterinarian for the most effectual vaccination schedule for your Norfolk Terrier puppy.

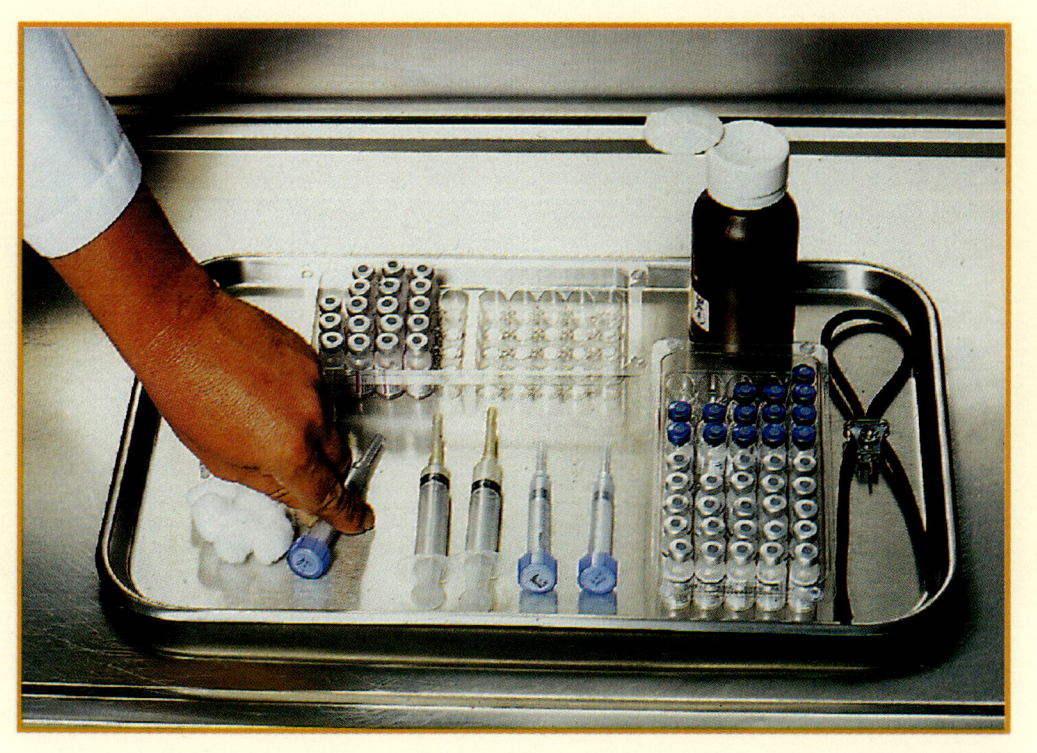

HEALTH

attacking bacteria. However, they must first recognize a potential enemy.

Vaccines are either dead bacteria or they are live, but in very small doses. Either type prompts the pup's defense system to attack them. When a large attack then comes (if it does), the immune system recognizes it and massive numbers of lymphocytes (white blood corpuscles) are mobilized to counter the attack. However, the ability of the cells to recognize these dangerous viruses can diminish over a period of time. It is therefore useful to provide annual reminders about the nature of the enemy. This is done by means of booster injections that keep the immune system on its alert. Immunization is not 100-percent guaranteed to be successful, but is very close. Certainly it is better than giving the puppy no protection.

Dogs are subject to other viral attacks, and if these are of a high-risk factor in your area, then your vet will suggest you have the puppy vaccinated against these as well.

Your puppy or dog should also be vaccinated against the deadly rabies virus. In fact, in many places it is illegal for your dog not to be vaccinated. This is to protect your dog, your family, and the rest of the animal population from this deadly virus that infects the nervous system and causes dementia and death.

ACCIDENTS

All puppies will get their share of bumps and bruises due to the rather energetic way they play. These will usually heal themselves over a few days. Small cuts should be bathed with a suitable disinfectant and then smeared with an antiseptic ointment. If a cut looks more serious, then stem the flow of blood with a towel or makeshift tourniquet and rush the pup to the veterinarian. Never apply so much pressure to the wound that it might restrict the flow of blood to the limb.

In the case of burns you should apply cold water or an ice pack to the surface. If the burn was due to a chemical, then this must be washed away with copious amounts of water. Apply petroleum jelly, or any vegetable oil, to the burn. Trim away the hair if need be. Wrap the dog in a blanket and rush him to the vet. The pup may go into shock, depending on the severity of the burn, and this will result in a lowered blood pressure, which is dangerous and the reason the pup must receive immediate veterinary attention.

HEALTH

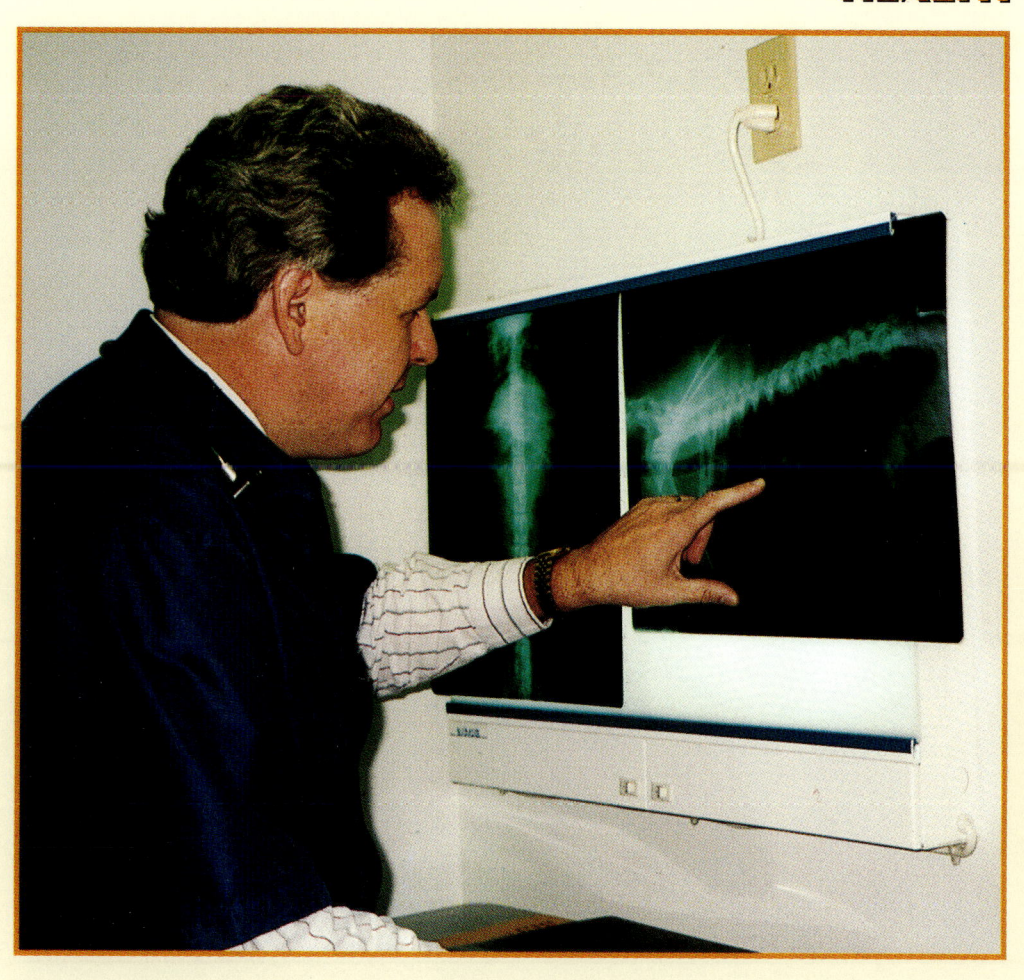

It is a good idea to x-ray the chest and abdomen on any dog hit by a car.

If a broken limb is suspected then try to keep the animal as still as possible. Wrap your pup or dog in a blanket to restrict movement and get him to the veterinarian as soon as possible. Do not move the dog's head so it is tilting backward, as this might result in blood entering the lungs.

Do not let your pup jump up and down from heights, as this can cause considerable shock to the joints. Like all youngsters, puppies do not know when enough is enough, so you must do all their thinking for them.

Provided you apply strict hygiene to all aspects of raising your puppy, and you make daily checks on his physical state, you have done as much as you can to safeguard him during his most vulnerable period. Routine visits to your veterinarian are also recommended, especially while the puppy is under one year of age. The vet may notice something that did not seem important to you.

CONGENITAL AND ACQUIRED DISORDERS

by Judy Iby, RVT

Veterinarians and breeders now recognize that many of the disease processes and faults in dogs, as well as in human beings, have a genetic predisposition. These faults are found not only in the purebred dog but in the mixed breed as well. Likely these diseases have been present for decades but more recently are being identified and attributed to inheritance. Fortunately many of these problems are not life threatening or even debilitating. Many of these disorders have a low incidence. It is true that some breeds and some bloodlines within a breed have a higher frequency than others. It is always wise to discuss this subject with breeders of your breed.

Presently very few of the hundreds of disorders can be identified through genetic testing. Hopefully with today's technology and the desire to improve our breeding stock, genetic testing will become more readily available. In the meantime the reputable breeder does the recommended testing for his breed. The American Kennel Club is encouraging OFA (Orthopedic Foundation for Animals) hip and elbow certification and CERF (Canine Eye Registration Foundation) certifications and is listing them on AKC registrations and pedigrees. This is a step forward for the AKC in encouraging better breeding. They also founded a Canine Health Foundation to aid in the research of diseases in the purebred dog.

Opposite: The responsible Norfolk Terrier breeder, understanding the potential problems within the breed, strives to produce healthy puppies and contribute to the betterment of the breed.

BONES AND JOINTS

Hip Dysplasia

Canine hip dysplasia has been confirmed in 79 breeds. It is the malformation of the hip joint's ball and socket, with clinical signs from none to severe hip lameness. It may appear as early as five months. The incidence is

CONGENITAL DISORDERS

CONGENITAL DISORDERS

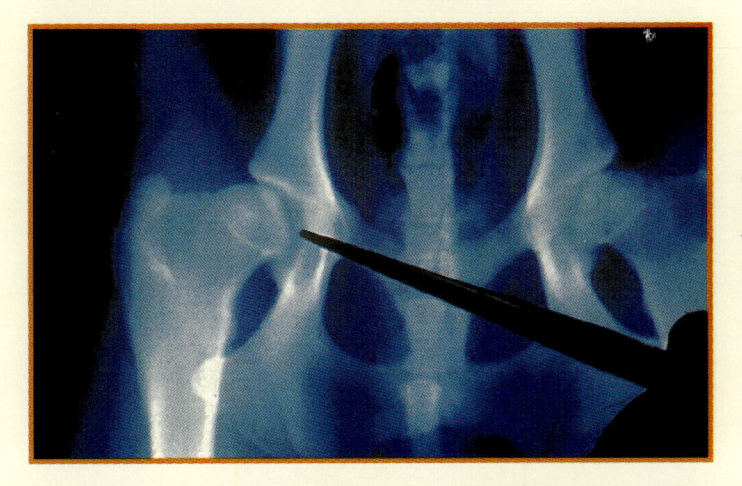

Radiograph of a dog with hip dysplasia. Note the flattened femoral head at the marker. Photo courtesy of Toronto Academy of Veterinary Medicine, Toronto, Canada.

reduced within a bloodline by breeding normal to normal, generation after generation. Upon submitting normal pelvic radiographs, the OFA will issue a certification number.

Elbow Dysplasia

Elbow dysplasia results from abnormal development of the ulna, one of the bones of the upper arm. During bone growth, a small area of bone (the anconeal process) fails to fuse with the rest of the bone. This results in an unstable elbow joint and lameness, which is aggravated by exercise. OFA certifies free of this disorder.

Patellar Luxation

This condition can be medial or lateral. Breeders call patellar luxations "slips" for "slipped kneecaps." OFA offers a registry for this disorder. Patellar luxations may or may not cause problems.

Intervertebral Disk Disease (IVD)

IVD is a condition in which a disk(s), the cushion between each vertebrae of the spine, tears and the gel-like material leaks out and presses on the spinal cord. The degeneration is progressive, starting as early as two to nine months, but usually the neurological symptoms are not apparent until three to six years of age. Symptoms include pain, paresis (weariness), incoordination, and paralysis. IVD is a medical emergency. If you are unable to get professional care immediately, then confine your dog to a crate or small area until he can be seen.

CONGENITAL DISORDERS

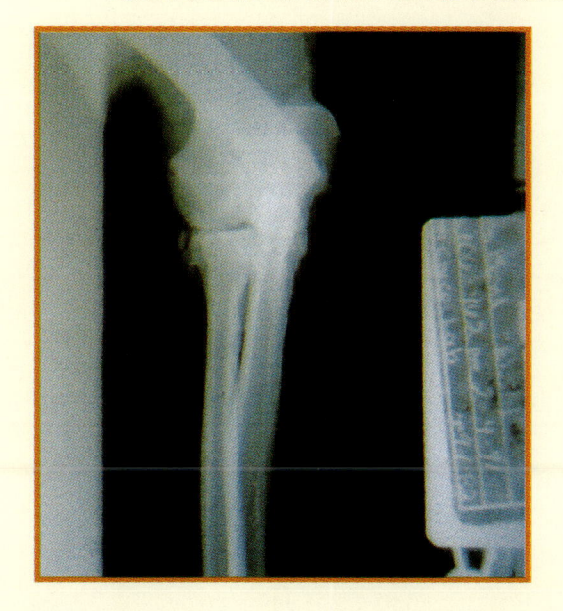

Fragmented coronoid process of the elbow, a manifestation of elbow dysplasia. Photo courtesy of Jack Henry.

Spondylitis
Usually seen in middle to old-age dogs and potentially quite serious in the latter, spondylitis is inflammation of the vertebral joints and degeneration of intervertebral disks resulting in bony spur-like outgrowths that may fuse.

CARDIOVASCULAR AND LYMPHATIC SYSTEMS

Dilated Cardiomyopathy
Prevalent in several breeds, this is a disease in which the heart muscle is damaged or destroyed to the point that it cannot pump blood properly through the body resulting in signs of heart failure. Diagnosis is confirmed by cardiac ultrasound.

Lymphosarcoma
This condition can occur in young dogs but usually appears in dogs over the age of five years. Symptoms include fever, weight loss, anorexia, painless enlargement of the lymph nodes, and nonspecific signs of illness. It is the most common type of cancer found in dogs. Chemotherapy treatment will prolong the dog's life but will not cure the disease at this time.

BLOOD

Von Willebrand's Disease
VWD has been confirmed in over 50 breeds and is

CONGENITAL DISORDERS

a manageable disease. It is characterized by moderate to severe bleeding, corrected by blood transfusions from normal dogs and frequently seen with hypothyroidism. When levels are low, a pre-surgical blood transfusion may be necessary. Many breeders screen their breeding stock for vWD.

Immune-Mediated Blood Disease

Immune-mediated diseases affect the red blood cells and platelets. They are called autoimmune hemolytic anemia or immune-mediated anemia when red blood cells are affected, and autoimmune thrombocytopenic purpura, idiopathic thrombocytopenic purpura, and immune-mediated thrombocytopenia when platelets are involved. The disease may appear acutely. Symptoms include jaundice (yellow color) of the gums and eyes and dark brown or dark red urine. Symptoms of platelet disease include pinpoint bruises or hemorrhages in the skin, gums and eye membranes; nosebleeds; bleeding from the GI tract or into the urine. Any of these symptoms constitutes an emergency!

DIGESTIVE SYSTEM AND ORAL CAVITY

Colitis

This disorder has no known cause and appears with some frequency in certain breeds. It is characterized by an intermittent bloody stool, with or without diarrhea.

Chronic Hepatitis

This is the result of liver failure occuring at relatively young ages. In many cases clinical signs are apparent for less than two weeks. They include anorexia, lethargy, vomiting, depression, diarrhea, trembling or shaking, excess thirst and urination, weight loss, and dark bloody stool. Early diagnosis and treatment promise the best chance for survival.

Copper Toxicity

Copper toxicity occurs when excessive copper is concentrated in the liver. In 1995 there was a breakthrough when the DNA marker was identified in one of the afflicted breeds. Therefore carriers will be identified in the future.

CONGENITAL DISORDERS

ENDOCRINE SYSTEM

Hypothyroidism
Over 50 breeds have been diagnosed with hypothyroidism. It is the number-one endocrine disorder in the dog and is the result of an underactive thyroid gland. Conscientious breeders are screening their dogs if the disease is common to their breed or bloodline. The critical years for the decline of thyroid function are usually between three and eight, although it can appear at an older age. A simple blood test can diagnose or rule out this disorder. It is easily and inexpensively treated by giving thyroid replacement therapy daily. Untreated hypothyroidism can be devastating to your dog.

Addison's Disease
Primary adrenal insufficiency is caused by damage to the adrenal cortex, and secondary adrenocortical insufficiency is the result of insufficient production of the hormone ACTH by the pituitary gland. Symptoms may include depression, anorexia, a weak femoral pulse, vomiting or diarrhea, weakness, dehydration, and occasionally bradycardia.

Cushing's Disease
Hyperadrenocorticism is the over-production of steroid hormone. Dogs on steroid therapy may show Cushing-like symptoms. Some of the symptoms are excess thirst and urination, hair loss, and an enlarged, pendulous, or flaccid abdomen.

EYES

Cataracts
Breeders should screen their breeding stock for this disorder. A cataract is defined as any opacity of the lens or its capsule. It may progress and produce blindness or it may remain small and cause no clinical impairment of vision. Unfortunately some inherited cataracts appear later in life after the dog has already been bred.

Lens Luxation
This condition results when the lens of the eye is not in normal position, and may result in secondary glaucoma.

CONGENITAL DISORDERS

Glaucoma

Primary glaucoma is caused by increased intraocular pressure due to inadequate aqueous drainage and is not associated with other intraocular diseases. It may initially be in one eye. Secondary glaucoma is caused by increased intraocular pressure brought on by another ocular disease, tumor, or inflammation.

Keratoconjunctivitis Sicca

"Dry eye" (the decrease in production of tears) may be the result of a congenital or inherited deficiency of the aqueous layer, a lack of the proper nervous stimulation of the tearing system, a traumatic incident, or drugs, including topical anesthetics (such as

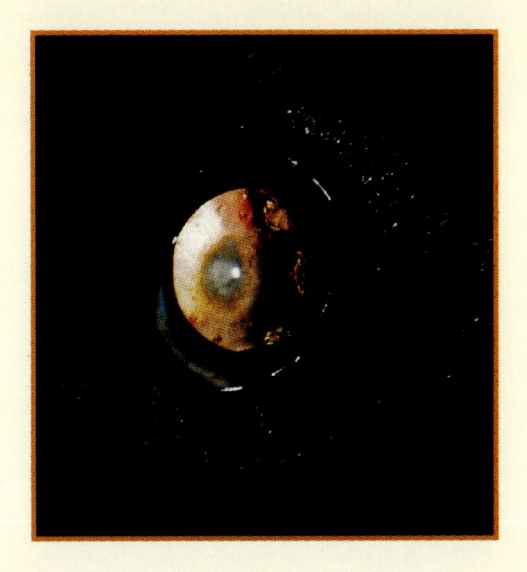

An immature cataract is evident in this dilated pupil. The central white area and cloudy areas at 4:00, 6:00 and 8:00 represent the cataract. Photo courtesy of Dr. Kerry L. Ketring.

atropine, and antibiotics containing sulfadiazine, phenazopyridine or salicyla-sulfapyridine). There seems to be an increased incidence of "dry eye" after "cherry eye" removal.

Progressive Retinal Atrophy (PRA)

This is the progressive loss of vision, first at night, followed by total blindness. It is inherited in many breeds.

Distichiasis

Distichiasis results from extra rows of eyelashes growing out of the meibomian gland ducts. This condition may cause tearing, but tearing may be the result of some other problem that needs to be investigated.

CONGENITAL DISORDERS

Entropion
Entropion is the inward rolling of the eyelid, usually lower lid, which can cause inflammation and may need surgical correction.

Ectropion
Ectropion is the outward rolling of the eyelid, usually lower lid, and may need surgical correction.

Hypertrophy of the Nictitans Gland
"Cherry eye" is the increase in size of the gland resulting in eversion of the third eyelid and is usually bilateral. Onset frequently occurs during stressful periods such as teething.

NEUROMUSCULAR SYSTEM

Epilepsy
Epilepsy is a disorder in which the electrical brain activity "short circuits," resulting in a seizure. Numerous breeds and mixed breeds are subject to idiopathic epilepsy (no explainable reason). Seizures usually begin between six months and five years of age. Don't panic. Your primary concern should be to keep your dog from hurting himself by falling down the stairs or falling off furniture and/or banging his head. Dogs don't swallow their tongues. If the seizure lasts longer than ten minutes, you should contact your veterinarian. Seizures can be caused by many conditions, such as poisoning and birth injuries, brain infections, trauma or tumors, liver disease, distemper, and low blood sugar or calcium. There are all types of seizures from generalized (the dog will be shaking and paddling/kicking his feet) to standing and staring out in space, etc.

UROGENITAL

Cryptorchidism
This is a condition in which either one or both of the testes fail to descend into the scrotum. There should not be a problem if the dog is neutered early, before two to three years of age. Otherwise, the undescended testicle could turn cancerous.

PET OWNERS & BLOOD PRESSURE

Over the past few years, several scientific studies have documented many health benefits of having pets in our lives. At the State University of New York at Buffalo, for example, Dr. Karen Allen and her colleagues have focused on how physical reactions to psychological stress are influenced by the presence of pets. One such study compared the effect of pets with that of a person's close friend and reported pets to be dramatically better than friends at providing unconditional support. Blood pressure was monitored throughout the study, and, on average, the blood pressure of people under stress who were *with* their pets was 112/75, as compared to 140/95 when they were with the self-selected friends. Heart rate differences were also significantly lower when participants were with their pets. A follow-up study included married couples and looked at the stress-reducing effect of pets versus *spouses*, and found, once again, that pets were dramatically more successful than other people in reducing cardiovascular reactions to stress. An interesting discovery made in this study was that when the spouse and pet were *both* present, heart rate and blood pressure came down dramatically.

Other work by the same researchers has looked at the role of pets in moderating age-related increases in blood pressure. In a study that followed 100 women (half in their 20s and half in their 70s) over six months, it was found that elderly women with few social contacts and *no* pets had blood pressures that were significantly higher (averages of 145/95 compared to 120/80) than elderly women with their beloved pets but few *human* contacts. In other words, elderly women with pets, but no friends, had blood pressures that closely reflected the blood pressures of young women.

This series of studies demonstrates that pets can play an important role in how we handle everyday stress, and shows that biological aging cannot be fully understood without a consideration of the social factors in our lives.

> More than best friends or even spouses, pets have a natural calming effect on their humans.

SKULL — Wide and slightly rounded.

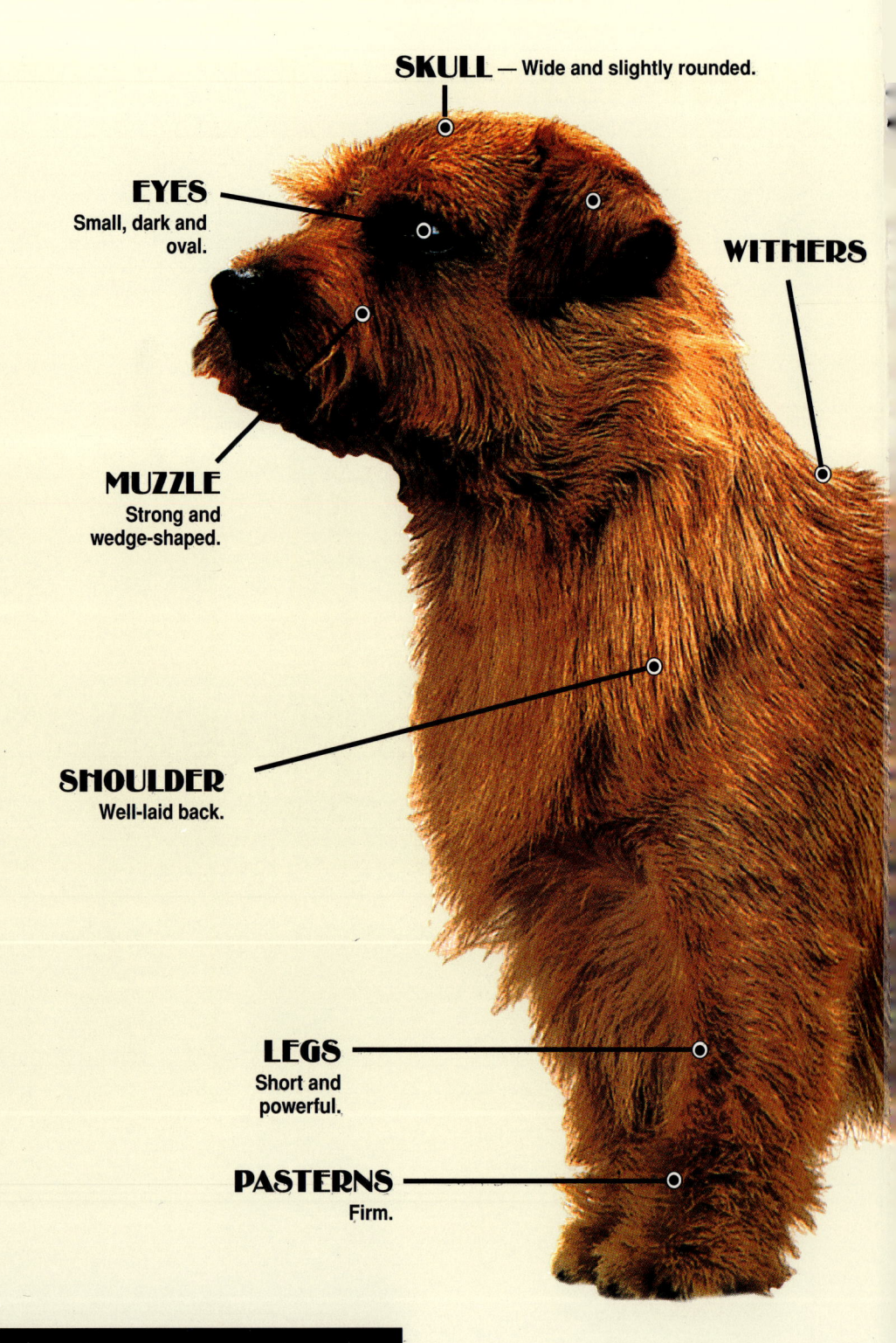

EYES
Small, dark and oval.

WITHERS

MUZZLE
Strong and wedge-shaped.

SHOULDER
Well-laid back.

LEGS
Short and powerful.

PASTERNS
Firm.

Ch. Max-Well's Weatherman owned by Mrs. Barbara Miller.